Helping Students Take Control of Everyday Executive Functions

of related interest

AD/HD Homework Challenges Transformed!
Creative Ways to Achieve Focus and Attention by Building on AD/HD Traits
Harriet Hope Green
ISBN 978 1 84905 880 3
eISBN 978 0 85700 601 1

Helping Kids and Teens with ADHD in School
A Workbook for Classroom Support and Managing Transitions
Joanne Steer and Kate Horstmann
Illustrated by Jason Edwards
ISBN 978 1 84310 663 0
eISBN 978 1 84642 923 1

Common SENse for the Inclusive Classroom
How Teachers Can Maximise Existing Skills to
Support Special Educational Needs
Richard Hanks
ISBN 978 1 84905 057 9
eISBN 978 0 85700 247 1

Addressing the Unproductive Classroom Behaviours of Students with
Special Needs
Steve Chinn
ISBN 978 1 84905 050 0
eISBN 978 0 85700 357 7

Helping Students Take Control of Everyday Executive Functions

PAULA MORAINE, M.ED.

Jessica Kingsley *Publishers*
London and Philadelphia

First published in 2012
by Jessica Kingsley Publishers
116 Pentonville Road
London N1 9JB, UK
and
400 Market Street, Suite 400
Philadelphia, PA 19106, USA

www.jkp.com

Library of Congress Cataloging in Publication Data
A CIP catalog record for this book is available from the Library of Congress

British Library Cataloguing in Publication Data
A CIP catalogue record for this book is available from the British Library

ISBN 978 1 84905 884 1
eISBN 978 0 85700 576 2

Printed and bound in the Great Britain

For the students—so your voices can be heard more easily.

Acknowledgments

This book evolved over my many years in education with students of all ages. There are too many people who gave me insight, guidance, and encouragement to list them all here. The students who inspired me are an even greater number. Some of them know who they are, while others would be astonished to hear that they made such an impression on me.

I am grateful to the students who were so eager for me to write this book, and who were so willing to let me share the experiences of our work together. While all the names have been changed, the students will easily recognize their own words. I have, whenever possible, faithfully reproduced their words exactly using notes and recordings.

A special acknowledgment goes to my colleagues at The Highlands School in Bel Air, MD, for their support of the new tutoring program, and their affirmation of my work to include the theme of executive function as an integral part of the mission of The Highlands School Community Outreach Center for Literacy and Tutoring Program.

Contents

Introduction

Attention—we all have it, and we are all affected by the way we use it. Attention of some kind is at the core of every waking experience. Over the years, I have asked people how they assess their own attention, and I get one of three common answers: that they think they have too much attention and can get hyper-focused; they have a deficit, or too little attention; or they have no idea because they have never thought about it. Not surprisingly, no one ever says they think of their attention as being "just right," or in perfect balance. Everyone feels their attention needs to be fixed, improved, or changed in some way.

This can be good news. Attention is an activity that is in constant movement; it does not stand still and cannot be fixed into place. It is similar to the swing of a pendulum that is always passing through the point of perfect balance on its way toward one side (or extreme) or the other. If we were to stop the pendulum in the middle, at the point of perfect balance, and fix it into place, all movement would have to stop in order for the pendulum to stay there. My understanding of attention is that if it would ever come to such a point of stillness, without movement, it would cease to be.

The challenge confronting teachers and parents can often be traced back to the challenge of attention. So how can we understand someone else's experience of attention well enough to be of help? Can we understand someone else's use of attention if we do not understand our own use of attention? Try this exercise that I frequently do with students, and see what happens for you. Close your eyes, and for 15 seconds, concentrate on absolutely nothing but a paper clip. No other thoughts, just focus on the paper clip. At the end of this very short exercise, I ask the student to tell me if it was possible for them to do it, and what happened when they tried. The most common answer is, "That was really hard!" At first, it sounded like it would be easy, and everyone starts off on the 15 seconds thinking that I am kind of silly for asking them to do this. After 15 seconds, they look at me and say it didn't work, and they want to know why it didn't work. With that question, we are ready to start our work together.

The reason why it is so hard to concentrate for 15 seconds on a paper clip is the same as the reason why it is so hard to bring our attention to that place of stillness, or perfect balance in the middle of the pendulum. By its very nature, attention does not want to be stopped. The individual who understands how to "ace" this exercise and make it work, knows how to gather all their attention and actively focus it on one spot. It seems like they have held their attention in a point of stillness, but it is rather more like a helicopter that hovers over the landing place without moving up or down. The physics of a helicopter requires it to move a little, even if it looks like it is not moving, so it can keep the right amount of air under the blades. If the helicopter does not move just a bit, it loses the air under the blades and crashes to the ground. The laws of attention are similar, in that attention has to be engaged in some kind of tiny movement at all times, or it will shut down. Therefore, in the concentration exercise, focusing attention on the paper clip requires some tiny "attention movement" in order both to stay with the picture of the paper clip, and not to let the mind wander to any other thought.

Try the exercise again now, for another 15 seconds. Even knowing what is behind the exercise, it is still hard to do, and our natural longing for attention that "moves" is strong. So it is very difficult, if not impossible, to fix our attention down to one thing exclusively. But does that necessarily mean that our attention is broken and needs to be fixed? Cathy Davidson (2011) discusses the new brain science of attention in her book *Now You See It*. After describing "attention blindness" from a multitude of perspectives, she eventually reminds the reader that the ways we pay attention now, in the 21st century, are different from the ways that previous generations paid attention; and that those old ways need not so much to be fixed, as to be changed. It is our understanding of attention that keeps getting stuck on old understanding, and that is what needs fixing.

We would all benefit from new insight into attention, from updated expectations about attention, and new attention skills.

This book addresses attention in context as one of the executive functions. It offers ideas for understanding, nurturing, and reviving executive function from the perspective of the parent, teacher, and the student. The examples in the book are taken mainly, but not exclusively, from the experiences of the school-aged student. As teachers and parents, we are constantly dealing with our own executive function, while simultaneously trying to educate our students and children so they can effectively develop their executive function. The goal of this book is to make the efforts of teachers and parents more meaningful for the sake of the student who is struggling to sort out how he or she learns best. In my work as a teacher, tutor, and educator, I find that when I turn my attention to the student, and listen carefully to what he or she has to say, that student gains a voice in their own education.

> I don't know why my grades are bad. I think I am doing pretty good. I could improve, but I am doing OK. I am doing good in science, but I could pay attention more.
> (13-year-old boy with executive function challenges)

This quote comes from an eighth grade student who is barely passing any of his classes. The most recent report from his teachers expresses great concern about his lack of focus and absence of motivation. This student is very smart and has a charming personality, but he is beginning to get depressed over the growing disconnect between what he feels he can do and the feedback from teachers indicating his very poor performance. In a recent assignment to write a persuasive essay about a personally chosen topic, he chose to write about "Chewing Gum in School." His assignment was to write an essay that would persuade the reader, based on the pros and cons of his topic. His main (and only) argument for chewing gum was that it felt good, and his main (and only) argument against chewing gum was that it annoyed the teachers. For him, this was a completed thought process and he figured it would be a good paper with these two arguments.

His teachers take extra time to explain assignments to him, give him clear directions, and set him clear time limits. They are willing to speak with his parents to strategize and discuss ideas that might help him. They recognize and acknowledge that he has some learning challenges based on organization, and are willing to adjust some of their expectations of him.

His parents are concerned because their interventions and efforts to help him have not been successful. They work with him every evening on his homework; they go through all his papers and help him organize his binder; they stay in close contact with his teachers so they have the updated assignments and expectations; they review his student planner each day; they provide him with special educational interventions in the form of private, individualized tutoring. What more can they do? Their son is growing discouraged, is upset by everything having to do with school, and doesn't understand why his work is being judged so poorly. In response, he tries to avoid thinking about school homework and exams. He perceives his parents' attempts to help him as nagging and excessive. Frequently, battles ensue, resulting in anger, frustration, and even tears for both this student and his parents. These emotionally charged interactions cause additional blows to his self-esteem and give him all the more reason to avoid schoolwork.

What is going on with this student? He has been diagnosed with executive dysfunction. His parents brought this diagnosis to the teachers, and had conversations with them, and tried to come to an understanding of what they could do to help him. This student is one of the lucky ones because he has parents who are informed, engaged, and willing to work together with his teachers to find solutions. His teachers are able and willing to put some accommodations in place during the school day.

Parents can turn to educational support services within the school structure, if such help is available. When it is not available at school, parents might turn to a tutor, an academic coach, or some other provision of educational intervention. I met many of the students described in this book when they came for individual tutoring in executive function. Other students in this book are from one of the classes, workshops, private consultations, or university courses

I have taught or presented over the years. The experiences of the students are real, as are their challenges, frustrations, efforts, and successes.

When parents and students come to me seeking help with executive function, they are often surprised that I do not immediately offer them a list of strategies to work on. I do not offer them a list of definitions for the executive functions, and I do not tell them what to do. Instead, I tell them that I will go through an individualized process with them, either with their student alone or with the parents joining us, and try to match the "ingredients" or tools described in this book to the area of executive function need. This sounds at first like a laborious process, but in fact it usually does not take too long before the important issues for an individual student are identified, the focus is narrowed down, and some creative results start appearing. We might not need to use every ingredient and we might not need to work directly on every one of the functions. The creative aspect comes in by using one or more of the ingredients to organize or strengthen one or more of the executive functions. Consider the image of a painter who has a palette of colors. The colors available to the painter might be the same colors any painter can use, but each artist will apply the colors in such a way that they produce a unique painting. The ingredients described in this book are like the colors of a painter's palette: each person has access to the ingredients, but how the ingredients are combined and applied is very individual, personal, and unique. By using these ingredients, teachers or parents can help the student gain access to the best, most appropriate, and highly personalized understanding of his or her executive function.

What is executive function?

Executive functions are the functions of our brain that control attention and behavior. Executive functions might be discussed from numerous perspectives and in various detail, but there is agreement that controlling attention and behavior is the brain's executive activity.

As you will read here, attention is one of the most fundamental tools that the learner has. The moment a teacher or a parent understands how the student or child uses attention, the path toward understanding how to manage executive functions has begun in earnest.

An extended list of executive functions might include:

- attention

- initiative

- inhibition

- flexibility

- shift

- planning

- organization

- time management

- memory

- working memory

- self-monitoring

- emotional control

- problem solving

- goal setting

- cognitive activation.

While there are numerous, lengthy working definitions available, more recent discussions regarding executive function tend to provide a much shorter, more condensed list of functions. Russell Barkley (2005), for example, defines executive function explicitly in relation to attention, referring to attention in terms of a relationship between environmental events and behavior. Environmental events are any events we experience with our senses, and behavior includes physical actions, cognitive activity (thinking), and inner actions (including feelings). In this context, attention can be seen as a relationship between an event and the response to that event. In that slight delay between event and response, our executive function is activated, and our behavior is a result of how we respond to the event.

In my work, I have the theoretical definitions available if teachers or parents are interested, but in daily contact with students I use descriptors that are related to practical experience. These descriptors arise out of my work with students of all ages, with teachers and colleagues, and with parents. Although this book is written primarily from my experience as a teacher, the conversation on behalf of the student is not complete without the insights and input from parents. The parent perspective will be included throughout in order to provide a full picture of the student's experience. The parenting and teaching roles can come very close together, and cooperative collaborations between teachers and parents engender the most successful outcomes.

My personal working definition of executive function is that we use our executive functions to express how we *think*, what we *feel*, and what we *do* in relation to the world around us. The way to a working definition of attention would be through understanding how we use our attention in our *thinking*, how we use our attention in relation to our *feelings*, and how we use our attention in our *actions*. It is my experience that students of all ages can understand how to use attention to strengthen executive functions if it is presented to them in this format.

How students relate to their environment is directly linked to their individual maturing process, so it is important to understand the development of executive function in the context of child development and the development of consciousness. We understand when a young child acts without thinking, initiates behaviors that have unexpected consequences, or does not exhibit reliable self-control at all appropriate times. We smile and often find such behavior charming. Forward a few years, and we are not so accepting of these behaviors when the child is in school. Children are expected to adjust to the structure and standards of the school day once they are around the age of six. By the time the child is in middle school (sixth through eighth grade), we can be seriously critical of the adolescent who acts without thinking through the consequences. The criticism increases through the teenage years as the gulf between expectations and behavior widens. It is natural to adjust expectations according to the assumed maturation and developmental age of the child, but in many cases, the child's brain development and behavior controls have not kept pace with their biological age. In these situations, we might expect certain results and specific behaviors from a child or young adult, but their capacity to meet these expectations is either slow in maturing, or is under-developed. The child is then accused of being unfocused, lazy, unmotivated, undisciplined, and unorganized, and the cycle of frustration, disappointment, and discouragement is established.

Executive functions develop slowly, reaching maturity only after nearly three decades. This means that our children, teenagers, and young adults are all in a maturing process, and so at any given moment are on a continuum of executive function development and maturity. So, knowing how often our expectations are out-of-sync with the reality, do we have the right understanding or attitude regarding the development and education of behaviors that are central to executive function? Do we explicitly teach children the skills needed to develop their executive functions in a systematic way? Do we match our expectations to the child's developmental level?

Too often we think that if we teach it, it is learned; if we said it, it was heard. How frustrating is it for teachers and parents to have to say the same thing over and over before the child seems to understand or respond? Most teachers will admit to self-doubt, questioning what they are doing wrong because the student does not seem to learn the "lesson" without multiple repetitions. Executive functions require time to evolve, develop, and mature, so keeping the long view in mind is important. A quick fix is usually not possible. Lessons will need repetition, and results will appear gradually.

Although we all learn about executive function in daily life, in the family setting, and via social norms, education requires that we explicitly teach executive function to the individual as well. How can we understand why this individualization is so necessary, and what can we do to make it happen? At a conference on leadership in education, one presenter quoted the American educator Roland

Barthes as saying that a leading thought for educators in all areas of pedagogical activity is that "we teach who we are." I understand this to mean that we teach from the center of who we are as an individual; we teach based on what we have achieved in our own path of maturing, evolving, and learning through life. Teachers know that students can always tell when they are faking it, or not being authentic. Who we are as a teacher is as important, if not more important, than what we know as a teacher. There is an interesting crossover truth between teachers and parents, because parents also "parent who they are." We live our life as a teacher or a parent as an expression of our life experience, education, and personality. How we make decisions in daily life is influenced by the totality of who we are, and our actions are formed and influenced by our core personality and beliefs. Many of us have the experience that "I have always been this way; these personality traits have been with me from early childhood."

After years of being inspired by the thought that we teach who we are, it suddenly dawned on me that our students and children also "learns who they are." Every person, young or old, is a unique individual as well as a unique learner. This fundamental principle can guide us in our search for each child's personal, individual, and unique learning style and learning needs. In a one-on-one setting, the one teacher or parent "teaches who they are" or "parents who they are" and the one student "learns who they are." In a classroom setting, the teacher is still an individual, while the students have become a group, a class, and each becomes one among many. So the teacher usually ends up teaching in one way to a group of very diverse learners. Teachers who are flexible by nature adapt their teaching to meet the needs of many learners. The flexible and adaptive teachers "teach who they are," and many students benefit. Less adaptive teachers, who can only teach essentially one way, also "teach who they are," but are usually able to reach only the few students who are like them.

"We learn who we are" is the principle that makes it so important that we educate the executive functions from the inside-out. Education cannot be applied from the outside like a coat of paint. The student cannot be commanded to learn based on outer structure, stringent testing systems, or even a universally established set of expectations. The student cannot learn by merely applying strategies to the situation, no matter how brilliant and appropriate those strategies might be. At some point, students need to experience their learning from the inside, awakening to the exciting experience that learning is interesting, even fun, and that they have some measure of control over the learning environment. If the interest to learn is awakened inside the student, it becomes much easier to find successful educational delivery systems. Once these principles are understood, each person can become his or her own best teacher.

Salutogenesis

Salutogenesis is another important principle, originally discussed by Aaron Antonovsky (1987) from a medical perspective which posits that there is a salutary, health causing factor that arises out of a sense of "coherence." Coherence in this context means that our experiences fit together, they are related, and, most important, they give us a feeling of being integrated. So, we feel well or healthy if we can make sense of our experiences, if our experiences are meaningful or valuable to us, and if we actually understand what is happening to us.

The same idea can be applied in education and leads to the questions, What is the health causing factor in education? What makes each of us a 'healthy' learner? How can we maintain health in our learning? These questions lead us to think about what makes us healthy, what makes learning successful, and why some achieve the sense of coherence or integration easily while others have to work so hard for it. These are crucial issues for teachers and parents to deal with on behalf of students.

What makes us healthy in education can be understood as an approach that seeks a healthy balance in learning; one that allows the student to learn in a coherent, integrated manner that supports resilience and healthy development. Antonovsky originally attributed the three components of comprehensibility, meaningfulness, and manageability to the sense of coherence. How are these three components experienced in education, and how do they ultimately lead to a sense of coherent, unified learning for the individual?

- *Comprehensibility:* Does the student understand/comprehend what is being asked of him or her? Does the student understand what is going on in general? Does the student have a sense of order or even predictability in his or her learning? Are the expectations clear?

- *Meaningfulness:* Does the student find the learning interesting and/or meaningful? Does the student care about the content being learned? Does the student find the experience of learning valuable or worth the effort? Is the learning relevant?

- *Manageability:* Does the student believe that he or she has the necessary skills, ability, and support to learn? Does the student experience the learning environment as one that is under control and manageable? Specifically, is the learning environment under the student's control? Does the student have the right tools for learning?

All too frequently, the student does not understand what is being asked of him or her. Even if the teacher tries to present material in an orderly and predictable manner, the student might still be confused. It is difficult for teachers to organize their teaching flexibly enough to accommodate each individual learning style and learning speed. It is therefore inevitable that the students in each class will have a variety of responses, based on individual skills and abilities.

Given the wide differences in any group of students, it is also to be expected that each student will find different content interesting or relevant. But every student needs to be able to care about learning, and ultimately each student needs to experience learning as valuable and worth the effort.

When the student goes home at the end of the day, the "homework nightmare" begins and parents have to sort out whether their child understands what is being asked of him or her. Too often, the only source of that information for the parents is the child, who may not have written anything down and does not remember what was said in class. If the child has difficulty even keeping track of assignments, then it is hard for the parents to be sure that the necessary tools are available to manage the work. Serious frustrations set in between the student and the parents over the homework. How can the parents help ensure that the learning is meaningful when they do not have access to it? What can they do to help their child maintain the link between schoolwork and homework if neither the parent nor the student can understand or communicate the meaningfulness of the schoolwork?

If we refer to the previous story of the eighth grade boy, it is clear from his comments that he actually understood the assignment, and understood what was being asked of him. The situation broke down because he did not find meaning or relevance in the assignment, and he was privately convinced that he was not going to be able to complete the work. He only had one of the three components of coherence (i.e. comprehension), so he made a bit of a joke of it, and said it was not important for him to do the work.

School hours are long, yet many essential life lessons do not fit into the time given for structured education. Parents have to take up where formal education left off and guide their children through the lessons of life. Therefore, the same questions are as relevant for the parents as they are for the teachers. Are these life experiences understandable, meaningful, and relevant? Does the child have the skills, tools, or context that will lead to success? Parents cannot rely on schools to provide a complete education for their children. Parents are faced with the need to teach many, many life lessons to their children, and this is, at times, a daunting task. A comment I hear frequently from parents is, "I just don't know what to do to help."

As a teacher, I find that working with parents and their children together can be very successful. Communication becomes easier because the child does not have to "report" back to the parents, relaying what we talked about. Adults also hear and understand different elements of the conversation than the child. Teachers and parents can be taught to be translators, and once they are able to interpret what their students/children are really saying to them, it will give the latter a greater sense of being heard and understood.

The need to experience a sense of coherence or integration is an "all the time" need. Coherence provides the learner with a sense of confidence, security, and purpose for living, not just academic learning. All of us need to be able to understand what is going on, to manage what is being asked of us, and to find meaning in our efforts. This leads each of us to a sense of coherence, unity, and connectedness that arises out of an experience of personal strength, which in turn leads to our feeling in control of our life and learning environment. It gives us a voice. My purpose with this book is to help teachers and parents give the student a voice.

When we approach education from the perspective of coherence, we start by identifying learning strengths rather than weaknesses, and learning abilities rather than disabilities. Education, which comes from the Latin "*educare*," "to lead out," has this gesture built into its very core. Our job as teachers is to continue to lead, to coax, and to cultivate the learner through his or her personal path of learning. The very nature of this approach to education is built on a sense of respect for the other, rather than a mission to change the other. As teachers and parents, we provide the tools, the structure, the guidance, and the environment, so that the students can "learn who they are."

Part I

Ingredients

The ultimate goal of this book is to make executive function more understandable and to provide a user-friendly model for teachers and parents. The approach used in this book is intended to create easy access to the somewhat confusing topic of executive function, and to give teachers and parents the necessary tools to guide students through an individualized approach to learning.

In Part I, eight ingredients or tools are presented that can be used to develop and strengthen the executive functions that are then described more thoroughly in Part II. The ingredients are:

1. relationship

2. strengths and weaknesses

3. self-advocacy to self-responsibility

4. preview and review: mental image

5. motivation and incentive

6. analysis and synthesis: from the whole to the parts and from the parts to the whole

7. rhythm and routine: practice and repetition

8. implicit and explicit.

Combinations of the ingredients can be used to enhance each executive function, so that the actual executive function becomes easier to use and apply in daily life. The same set of ingredients can be put together in many different ways to create many different outcomes. If we return to the analogy of the palette of colors, we see that even if every artist has the same colors available, the way the colors are used results in a different painting every time. Using the analogy of ingredients, consider that a cook may have flour, sugar, water, salt, and eggs available. These ingredients can be combined in endless ways to create cake, cookies, pancakes, crust, and bread, or as toppings, binders, fillers, and stuffing. It depends on the creativity of the cook and how the cook chooses to use the ingredients. What the cook wants to make and what ingredients the cook has available will determine the outcome. Continuing with the cooking example, we know that some cooks only want to follow a recipe, while others like to cook by "feel," creatively trying out new combinations and new ideas. Both approaches to cooking work well, but either way, the cook needs to understand the ingredients. These contrasting approaches can be expressed through the following two questions:

- What can you make with the ingredients you have?
- What do you want to make and what ingredients do you need to make it?

Do you decide what you are going to make, then go and gather the ingredients you need? Do you see the ingredients on the table and decide what creative concoction you can make with them? Do you use a cookbook and recipes, or do you cook by feel?

Whichever way you work, the material presented in this book can be used to enhance and clarify the executive functions by providing you with the necessary tools, ingredients, and options as a teacher or a parent to strengthen and improve the way your student's executive brain functions. This book will enable you to use these ingredients in combinations that are right for your student, help you provide insight into each student's personal, individual use of executive function, and give you new ways to integrate your student's attention with his or her personal strengths and capacities.

I know nothing about executive functions. I know I have had ADHD since it was diagnosed when I was five, but no one has ever told me about executive dysfunction. When I was in public school, I didn't know why I couldn't do as much as the other students could. Then when I went to a private school, I was guided through everything. I loved that school, but I didn't learn how to manage my time or organize my stuff—you know, the basics. Now I am in college and I read books, and for some reason I don't understand what I am reading. It is embarrassing that I don't know how to study, take notes, or even highlight what I need. Or maybe they taught me and I just didn't get it. So now I need to learn how to do it for real. (18-year-old college student)

Students of all ages need help and guidance in executive function, similar to the student quoted here. Most students have never heard of executive function, and although they might have received good, even excellent, instruction throughout the school years, they might not know how to guide their learning experience independently. This student was helped throughout her high-school years by her parents and her teachers. She had been given continued support, encouragement, and guidance. But, she arrived in college and was not able to translate all that help into successful, independent learning. Her parents are not pleased because they feel she has had an inordinate amount of extra help. Her teachers are not happy because they thought they had given her all the strategies she needed to be a successful student. She is not happy with herself because she feels she is letting everyone down and feels like she is just a big disappointment in general. Her parents want her to get help, but something that is different from the kind of support she has already received. They are looking for help to guide their daughter through the process of developing and/or upgrading her executive function capacities.

Some parents and students find their way to some kind of skilled educational intervention, while others have to try and figure out how to help the student without a tutor or educational guidance. Teachers may or may not have skilled colleagues to turn to for help, or programs in their school that can meet the needs of students with executive function challenges. For those teachers and parents who are working independently to better understand executive function, and how they can help students improve it, this book can serve as a guide.

CHAPTER 1

Relationship

- What is the student's relationship to the people around him or her?

- How do the student's relationships affect his or her learning?

- How can you work with these relationships in a way that supports the student's confidence and sense of self?

The first ingredient involves the student understanding the relationships in their situation. What is their relationship with the people who are helping them? How do they characterize their relationship with their parents? How are their relationships with their teachers? How are their relationships with friends? Most importantly, what is their relationship with themselves?

The key to all good relationships is trust. Does the student trust his or her parents, teachers, classmates? Do they trust in themselves? If people have let them down, or actively criticized them for not being successful, then trust in the other person or trust in oneself is damaged.

> Katy is a beautiful, energetic, entertaining young woman who has struggled with executive function difficulties her whole life. She found out when she was younger that she had ADHD, and has been provided with learning accommodations for many years. She came for help because her first year of college was not going well. She was turning her work in late, she was not studying effectively for exams, and she realized that it was

really hard to study on her own. Katy told me about all these problems, and was not happy to be meeting with me because she thought I was going to tell her to use a planner, take notes, and highlight her textbooks. But I did not do that. Instead, I asked her to describe her relationships. She was somewhat stunned by this question and thought I was joking. I convinced her that we would get back to all the studying details, but that I wanted her to describe her relationships with her family, friends, and herself first. She enthusiastically described her relationship with her friends. She has at least two very close friends and she elaborated on the friendship with colorful detail. She really, really likes these people and is very dedicated to her friendship with them. Her relationship with her family received mixed reviews. It is good, but she is beginning to move on with her life, and her bond with family members is starting to transform. But the bottom line in her relationship to her family is that she is grateful for all their support. Her relationship to herself is not that good. She is not happy about who she is, does not like herself, and asked that we not talk about her. She feels she is not interesting.

Now we are at the core issue! I turned her attention back to her loving and charming description of her two friends. I drew a circle, and put two stars on the circle, while restating her description of the two friends who are wonderful both for her and for each other. Then I put a black "X" on the circle to mark herself as the one friend in the circle not worthy of being a friend, who kind of stinks, and is not interesting. Her friends are so wonderful, and bring their "stars" to the circle of friends, and all she offers them is a big, black "X?" She looked genuinely surprised when I said this to her. So I asked her what she thought might be wrong with this picture? Eventually, we got around to realizing that she has a great deal to offer, and that being so negative about herself and claiming she has no redeeming qualities was neither accurate nor fair. It was not fair to her, and it certainly was not fair to her two wonderful friends. This led into an important conversation about the starting point being what she could do to strengthen her own relationship with herself.

If it is difficult for students to feel good about themselves in the context of a loving circle of friends, then how much more difficult must it be for them to feel safe and secure in a classroom situation where the student is one among many? The student must now respond to expectations and demands set by someone else (the teacher) in a situation that he or she may or may not like (the school). It is very difficult for students to separate out their feelings about themselves as distinct from the situation they are in at school. Most often, these two are completely merged. "I don't like school. I don't like myself." These two statements become tightly linked, even though it is comparing apples to oranges. The students' relationship to school is their relationship to a specific structure of learning, and an objective set of standards. Their relationship with themselves is an intimate, personal, and evolving bond that no one else can experience. It is private. So it is important to help the student have an independent experience of self that is not overwhelmed by their experience of school.

Helping the student gain confidence in their own relationship with themselves is most effective if it can be done in a somewhat private and protected setting, but a great deal can also be done toward this in the classroom setting. Ideally, the role of the teacher in school is to remove hindrances so the student can learn through inquiry and self-discovery—two excellent tools for self-knowledge and self-directed learning. Sadly, this too rarely happens. More frequently, students find the classroom situation to be one in which they are required to follow rules without question, learn facts as dictated by a set curriculum, and take tests that are written in a one-size-fits-all format.

What are we teaching our students in terms of relationships in a situation like the one described? Is this a picture of self-inquiry or self-discovery? Students who can follow rules, learn facts, and successfully take standardized tests might also have an easy relationship with the teachers and in most cases with their parents, due to the fact that the objective criteria in school are being met. But what about the student who doesn't easily follow rules, learn facts, or succeed at standardized testing? These students are labeled fairly quickly as difficult, non-compliant, and frequently failing students. So how is their relationship to the teachers now? How is their relationship to themselves? How is their confidence level? Whom do they trust? Parents become worried and might try various strategies to get their student to succeed. Teachers and parents both tell the student to apply more effort to their work. In quick order, the student has a broken relationship with the teacher, who will only give good feedback when the class rules are successfully followed; a strained relationship with his or her parents, who want their son or daughter to be successful but often do not know how to make it happen; and a great big dose of self-loathing and self-criticism for not being the kind of person who can meet all these expectations.

> John is a quiet, respectful eighth grade boy who is having some challenges in school but wants to learn how to be a better student because he is trying to get into a good high school. This is how he described his various relationships:
>
> *Teachers*: "My relationships with my teachers are not so strong, because when I am talking with my friends, they try to stop me. The teachers have gotten to where they don't believe the girls do anything wrong; they always believe it is the boys who do everything and the boys get in trouble. They are kind of sexist; it is difficult to trust them."
>
> *Parents*: "I have a strong relationship with my parents because I know that even if I do bad on something, they will always believe in me and never give up. I can always ask my parents for help because they know me so well. They know how I think and they can help me see what is the best thing for me to do."
>
> *Friends*: "I really have a strong relationship with some of them. We always have each other's backs."

Not all students can articulate their relationships as well as John does. This is a composite of the varied answers I more commonly receive from students:

- "My teachers don't know me at all."
- "My parents are just mad at me all the time. They think I am not trying, but I am."
- "My friends are the only ones who understand me."

Students frequently describe having a high level of trust in their friends, nearly no trust in their teachers, and mixed feelings about their relationship with parents. The "sense of self" is still developing for younger students, so they really do not know how they relate to themselves; the teenaged, high-school student is pretty convinced that no one really understands them; and the young adult is often bewildered at how hard it is to make a good relationship with anyone.

Fast forward the student into adult life, and similar strained relationships exist. The adult who still has not established a good relationship with him or herself might struggle in relationships with friends and partners, and will struggle in the workplace if confronted with expectations that cannot be met.

The remedy for such a multitude of strained relationships is both simple and very difficult: start small and begin by establishing one relationship that can be trusted. That might be with a single teacher, a tutor, a coach, a friend, or a parent. It only matters that the relationship contains trust, appreciation, and interest. If such a relationship is modeled to the student, it is more likely the student will at least have an idea of where to start in order to transform what is learned into a better relationship to self. Not all relationships can be changed, and certainly not all at once. The better your relationship is to yourself, the more likely it is that you can learn through the process of discovery within yourself.

Justin is a 16-year-old boy with a long history of learning challenges due to ADHD, dysgraphia, and written expression difficulties. He comes for tutoring and explicit help with executive function challenges. After an initial introduction, the following conversation sets the tone for further conversations.

"Hi, Justin, can you tell me something about what you are experiencing in school?"

"School is stupid. My teachers are stupid."

"Can you give me some details?"

"I dunno know."

And so the conversation proceeded for a bit longer, with "I dunno know" as the answer to each question. It became clear that he had no reason to trust me, or to care to share with me about anything. After all, I was the tutor, which is the same as being a teacher, and I could easily be just one more person in a long line of people who let him down. He wasn't going to let that happen.

"Justin, I am declaring an 'IDK-Free Zone' here."

"What's that?"

"An 'I dunno know-free zone.'"

"So."

"Anytime you don't know the answer to a question I ask, just say the words 'I don't know' and I will be happy to accept that answer."

"OK—it's kinda stupid, but OK."

And with that, we were able to start a relationship built on this one, small agreement. I held to my part of the agreement by saying "IDK-Free" whenever he said, "I dunno know" and that consistent, albeit very tiny decision, was enough to begin establishing trust. I continued to listen carefully to what he said, and I offered help whenever he was open to it. I made it clear that he was not there to please me but that I trusted him to let me help him in whatever way he needed. He needed time to test me and made me prove to him over and over again that I could be trusted, but eventually he relaxed and began to feel very different about his work and his abilities. By allowing himself to have a trusting relationship with me, he began to trust himself more in the process. One experience of trust made him susceptible to more experiences of trust. Trust can be contagious.

Start small—change one thing at a time! This is an important principle. If you want to be successful, only try to change one thing at a time. Relationships with other people grow, develop, and evolve—all words that indicate that change happens over time. Katy can build on the strength of her relationship with her friends and gradually grow the trust she has in others so that it includes trust in herself. Change can be slow, but it can give you hope. Every successful change makes you stronger for the next change and builds confidence needed for the future, and consequently for future changes. Once this pattern is established it tends to keep on going, and growing, and we keep changing.

After the initial conversation about relationships, I ask the student to fill out the form at the end of this chapter. This can be a very revealing exercise for him or her. As the teacher, fill one out for yourself—you might be surprised what you learn about your own relationships! I have noticed that parents often have a much more difficult time than the students in filling out this form. They will smile, say this is hard, and glance up to see their son or daughter busily filling out their form. That usually gets the parent writing—after all, if their child can do it, they can, too. The reason this kind of characterization is difficult for adults is partly because it requires some self-reflection, but primarily because it relies on self-knowledge. I always tell the adult that their answers can be private. The most important part of this little exercise is that they actually think about their relationships with others and with themselves. Teachers and parents can fall into the same kind of thinking that Katy did—expecting others to have good relationship with them, despite the fact that they may not have a very good relationship with themselves.

- Discover what the student's relationship is to the people around him or her.

- Start with small changes that are based on trust, and remind the student that the most important relationship they have is the relationship to themselves.

- Relationships built on trust are contagious!

Characterize your relationships with:

Yourself
Parents
Teachers
Friends
Family
Other (coach, extra-curricular activity leader, etc.)

Which relationships work the best for you, and why?

. . . .

. . . .

. . . .

. . . .

CHAPTER 2
Strengths and Weaknesses

- What is the student good at doing?

- What comes easy and what is difficult for him or her?

- What can be done to help empower a student and encourage their strengths?

Identifying a student's strengths and weaknesses comes at the beginning of the process of educating and improving the executive functions and is very connected to the relationship the student has with him or herself. I do not start the process by specifically identifying the student's weaknesses, because their weaknesses have been placed in too prominent a position for too long already. In general, most of us already hold on to our weaknesses more tightly. How many of us remember a criticism for ten years, but hold onto praise for only about an hour? It is a curious human trait to feel criticism more deeply than praise, to remember criticism longer, and to be more influenced by our perceived weaknesses than by our strengths. But criticism makes us feel terrible. We are so busy feeling awful that we rarely see the lesson the criticism was intended to impart. Here is another curious human trait—if criticism is not an effective teacher for us personally, why do we think that if we criticize someone else, they will be able to learn from it? It seems so simple when it is put like that, but it is so hard to remember when we are busily engaged in being irritated with the person we are eagerly criticizing.

Our educational system is structured on an inherent criticism scale in the form of a graded or pass/fail system. Students who do not get the grade they were hoping for feel criticized or demoralized by the lower grade. How many people do you know who are motivated by failure, or who strengthen their resolve to do better after having their weaknesses pointed out to them? The intention of testing is to reveal what is learned, yet the student's experience of being tested rarely has that result. The students I work with tend to look at their grades and see what they did not achieve, rather than what they did achieve. They experience testing as a criticism of what they did not accomplish, of what they did not learn, and of how badly they failed.

Most teacher–student or parent–student discussions do not include an insightful consideration of strengths. Students are rarely asked, "What are you good at doing?" "What do you like to do?" or "What is your natural approach to learning?" One student might be good with computers, another might be strong in math, be great at writing, or be good at art. What if the student does not have strengths in academic or school-related subjects, but is good at being a friend, or is good with animals, or is great at a sport? These are legitimate strengths and need to be acknowledged. A conversation about strengths can be a powerful experience for students, and gives them a chance to think about their learning from a new perspective. If you, as the teacher, can hold back and not talk about their weaknesses right away, students will have a chance to experience something good about being who they are. It does not matter if the strength is a natural strength the student was born with, or is a strength he or she worked to develop—starting from a position of strength will better ensure a more positive result.

Nathan is a fifth grade student having difficulty with reading comprehension and getting his thoughts down on paper. In our first session, his mother described some harsh comments made by his teachers and expressed her concern that he was being made to feel so bad about himself that his interest in learning was suffering. We settled into reading together, and we talked about the characters and events in the story. I would ask Nathan to tell me details about the story that impressed him. He was so engaged in trying to answer the way he thought I expected him to, that he did not really hear the story for himself. He said he was sorry every time I asked another question, assuming the reason I asked was because he did not answer correctly the first time. We then moved on to writing some of the ideas down, creating a personalized approach to a graphic organizer that allowed him to identify what was salient to him. He would write sentences and then say he was sorry when I read them, even though his writing was excellent. By the end of the first session, we made an agreement that he did not ever need to say "sorry" or "I'm sorry" in our sessions. He was saying "sorry" so frequently that I had to wonder how such a wonderful student could have been made to feel so sorry about so many things in just a few years of school. He had no idea what he could do well, since that idea had never been cultivated for him.

So, in the tutoring sessions, we started with his strengths, one of which happened to be an enormous vocabulary. He could come up with amazing descriptors and his choice of words went well beyond his grade level. By building on that strength, we reapproached his areas of challenge, and worked on a sequential, picture-forming approach to comprehension, using the key-word descriptors as a guide. Suddenly, he was able to comprehend better, as well as develop a descriptive paragraph that captured all the important points of the story. Later, we moved on to creative writing pieces, and "sorry" has nearly vanished from our conversations.

Working from one's strengths is not easy. First, we have to get to know our own strengths, requiring self-knowledge and insight that develop very slowly throughout our lifetime. Next, we have to be able to differentiate the kind of strengths we have in order to decide which strength is needed in a given situation. In the book *Your Child's Strengths*, Jenifer Fox (2009) describes the developmental areas of strength as a triad: activity strengths, learning strengths, and relationship strengths. Another way of saying this appears several times in this book: what are your strengths in thinking, feeling, and doing? Then, finally, we need to know how to apply the right strength in the right situation, or match the strength to the situation.

Consider the original goal of cohesion and it becomes easier to see why it is important to identify where a student is experiencing their strengths. If the student experiences *comprehensibility*, the strength might be in areas such as reading comprehension, listening to verbal directions, understanding content and context, and understanding theorems in math. If experiences are *meaningful*, the student is experiencing strengths in the realm of feelings, emotions, and relationships. The content of lessons in school can be understood in relation to personal interests and/or capacities. This might show as strength in imaginative thinking, or being able to relate personally to the images, and to imagine what lies behind the facts of a story or lesson. The students who have strengths in *manageability* can deal with the tactical demands of the situation. They can accomplish the task, organize the information, deal with the various requirements of student life, such as reading, writing, researching in different forms, organizing information, taking notes, highlighting important information, keeping a written record of assignments, recording assignments, managing time, etc. This begins to demonstrate that the student might have strengths in the area of cognition (or thinking), of meaningfulness (or feeling), and of manageability (or actions).

Students can also have strengths in each of these areas that have absolutely nothing to do with schoolwork. A student might find the world comprehensible through the ability to understand how things work, or how to program a computer. He or she might find meaningfulness in a project or service activity that meets the needs within the local community. An individual might be able to manage the work on a horse farm, or as a builder, and be reliable, consistent, and skilled in the kind of work that can never be proven on a standardized test. The real task here is to identify his or her areas of strength. Students know what their strengths are, but often no one has given them permission to enjoy their ability to program a computer as a cognitive strength, or identify the fact that they can be a good friend and recognize this as a strength in the area of emotions.

As we establish this list of ingredients, it will be clear that there are strengths to be found in each ingredient. How the student uses these ingredients, alone or in combination, will reveal more and more strengths, so that eventually the student will have a huge array of options available to work with. One of the most surprising things my students discover is that they each have more strengths, and a greater variety of strengths, than they ever imagined.

The conversation about strengths comes up very early in my conversation with students. Can they tell me one thing they think is a personal strength? Often they look at me with bewilderment because they have never thought of their strengths as something they could name or talk about. Some students believe they are not good at anything, while others might think their strengths are in a specific area, but there is no evidence to confirm it. There is too often a fairly big disconnect between what the student experiences as a strength and what can be objectively identified as true. Closing that gap, connecting the student's experience with reality, and establishing useful insight into their strengths can be empowering and encouraging.

Here are a few conversations that reveal how much a student might know about their strengths.

"Andrew, what would you say you are good at? What do you think are your strengths?"

"I don't know, I don't really have any."

"What do you do well enough to enjoy doing it?"

"Computers, I guess."

"What is it about computers you are good at?"

"Games."

"What kind of games?"

"The ones where you play with your friends online."

"Do you win?"

"No, it doesn't matter if I win, because I don't always want my friends to lose. We kind of take turns winning, so everyone gets a chance to win."

"So it is important to you that you and your friends care about each other?"

"Yeah, it wouldn't be fun if someone got mad because they always lose."

"So, would you say you are pretty good at being a friend?"

"I hadn't thought of it like that, but yeah, I am pretty good at that."

Another kind of strengths conversation went like this:

"Matt, what are you good at? What are your strengths?"

"Sports, I am good at sports."

"In what way are you good at sports?"

"Well, when I first started playing basketball I tried not to get down on myself because I wasn't very good at it. I wanted to do good for my friends. After a while, I did get better, and I guess I am just good at it now."

"Are you good at anything else besides sports?"

"I like Social Studies a lot, but I am not really good at it. I get mixed up when the test comes because I can't remember all the details."

"What do you like about Social Studies?"

"I like to picture what we are learning about."

"Do you mean you make pictures in your head about the lesson?"

"Yeah, and that makes it seem more real."

"But you still have trouble with remembering details on tests?"

"Yeah."

"So, how can you use your strengths in Social Studies to help you?"

"Well, can I do the picture thing?"

The answer is yes, of course. This student can be guided to use his strength in making pictures about the content and can be shown a few ways this might work. He can be shown how to draw a storyboard and track the content in pictures that way. He might be shown how to illustrate his notes. He might establish a system of symbols and colors to help him connect the facts to a picture in his mind. The system he uses is not the real point; finding access to his strengths in a way that inspires him to use his strengths is what will make him successful.

These conversations are representative of the nature of conversations I have with students. We start speaking about what the student thinks that he or she is good at (computer games, sports), and find out that the real strength lies in another area (friendship, learning through pictures). Every conversation I have with students about strengths typically ends in a different area than where it began. I enter these conversations willing to translate, and not take the students' first comments too literally. This kind of active, creative listening requires flexibility on the part of the parent, teacher, or tutor, and a willingness to read between the lines. I enter these conversations with no pre-conceived notions about what the student "should" say; they do not have to please me. They are free to simply state what they experience as true, and through conversation we can evolve and develop what they share into wonderful insights.

- Identify what a student's strengths are in relation to thinking, emotions, and skills.

- Empower and encourage the student through recognizing their strengths in more than purely academic areas.

- Provide opportunities for the student to work from their strengths, and build on success.

CHAPTER 3

Self-Advocacy to Self-Responsibility

- How do you learn to advocate for yourself?

- What do you need as self-awareness in order to identify your needs?

- How do you communicate your needs, once you recognize what your needs are?

We encourage self-advocacy in students, but what is self-advocacy? The term is often used to mean the way individuals with learning differences can speak up for themselves. In order to speak up for their needs, what do students first need to know about themselves before they can communicate it to others?

In the context of this book, I use the more literal meaning of the word advocacy, which means "to give support." Parental advocacy begins at birth, with the parent responding to all the needs of the child. Initially, the parent notices all the signals from the baby, and answers them accordingly. Gradually, the parents teach the pre-school child to communicate when they are hungry, tired, hot or cold, happy, or sad. This becomes a more defined system of communication when the child enters school. Suddenly, in school, it does not really matter if the child is hungry, unless it is time for a snack or lunch break. If it is not the "right" time, the child has to learn to put that specific need aside and relate instead to the needs and demands of the lesson. The self-advocacy he or she has previously learned is only relevant in school as long as it relates to the academic setting and the new rules set by teachers and other adults who don't really know the individual child. Now, all the child's needs related to the need to move, eat, rest, etc., are required to adapt directly to the rules of the academic learning environment. We do not teach a universal form of self-advocacy in our schools, but offer instead a rather restricted and limited range of options for sharing one's need.

To advocate is an act of will, so to teach self-advocacy is to teach a child to act on their own behalf, based on what they have learned through the process of self-discovery. In most situations, students are busy trying to figure out how to deal with the demands and expectations of the given situation, but there is little direct instruction focused on teaching them how to advocate for their personal or learning needs. A student is often just trying to make life manageable through communicating personal needs, yet it is not always possible to individualize the environment in order to meet those needs. Too often, a student will try to communicate a need, and they will be told to stop disturbing the class. They quickly learn that speaking up and asking questions results in a negative response, so they shut down and stop trying to self-advocate. Some adults perceive self-advocacy as self-indulgent behavior. Students are told that their needs can only be met if everyone in the class gets the same treatment. Instead of teaching students how to look out for each other and be sensitive to the needs of others, they are taught to not draw attention to themselves by advocating for what they need to learn. Students describe how it feels when they try to speak up for themselves and they get in trouble for it.

> Whenever I raise my hand to ask a question, or to ask for the notes so I can get my work done, I am told to stop disrupting the class. So, whatever, I just put my head down on the desk. Then the teachers tell me my "bad behavior" is a problem for them.

This student is accused of being non-compliant and that his "behavior" issues are the core of the problem. He has an Individual

Learning Plan (IEP) that clearly states that specific accommodations are to be provided, yet every time this student requests the items from his IEP, such as notes from the class or the assignment rubric, he is told he is being disruptive and that his behavior is bad. Parents get understandably frustrated in these moments because their child, as well as being denied the help he or she needs, is also accused of being the problem.

It is difficult for teachers, too, since there are many excellent teachers who try to meet the individual needs of the individual student, but who are required to work within the structure of their school system. Teachers also have to deal with the fallout resulting from the difficulties or negativity the student carries over from any previous teacher. It is a challenging environment in which to teach the student self-advocacy, but, while it is true that no social system can work well if every person acts only in their own best interest, a great social/educational system would take individual needs into account as fully as possible and try to find some common ground to share.

Students, even those who have experienced negativity when they have tried to self-advocate, can and should be led in a personal exercise of self-reflection by addressing these questions related to building up and establishing self-advocacy:

- What are my needs?

- How do I learn?

- What can I do to make learning work better for me?

- What is one thing I can do to advocate for myself?

Initially, when you ask a student to answer these questions, they will have no idea what you are talking about. I was very impressed one day when a mother brought her son in for tutoring and she told this eighth grade boy to tell me what he needed, since he had been taught to self-advocate. As soon as she said this, however, her son looked very uncomfortable, squirmed a little, and said, "But I don't know what I need." So he had been taught about self-advocacy, but he had not learned how to fully engage with it yet. At least he had an idea of what it was, so we began by reconstructing what he did know about self-advocacy and what he knew about his own learning. I was still impressed, because he had been introduced to the idea of thinking about his own needs, and that made him more able to engage in a conversation with me.

Self-advocacy requires self-knowledge, which only evolves with maturity. Teachers, as they relate to the group, have a general expectation of how much self-knowledge students in a specific grade level can be expected to have. Most parents have a good idea of their individual child's maturity level, and therefore will know how much self-knowledge they can expect. In the best case scenario, parents and teachers are able to provide a protected structure in which the child gradually learns to speak up for his or her needs, while at the same time learning about how to respect the needs of others.

Maturity is expressed in how the child's awareness of the world around him or her changes. Young children begin by being aware of "self"—how they feel, if they are hungry, cold, happy, etc. Their entire experience of the world and all the sensory input that comes to them from the world is experienced in relation to themselves. Later, as they grow older, their experience is broadened by becoming aware of the "other," of those around them and what their needs are. The movement from self-awareness to awareness of the other is only possible through maturity. The younger the child, the better they are at self-advocating, long before anyone teaches them what that term means. Imagine the baby, crying or screaming because it is hungry—that is self-advocacy in its purest form! Later, this natural self-advocacy fades because the child needs to learn social skills, manners, and self-control. The seven-year-old child is not allowed to scream just because he or she is hungry. The adult is expected to find appropriate social moments to mention that it might be a good time for a nap. The natural, automatic, and unconscious self-advocacy skills of early childhood require adaptation in order to become the socially acceptable, controlled, and conscious self-advocacy skills of the older child or young adult.

We understand that self-advocacy and maturity cannot be taught one day and tested the next. We also understand that even if a child is mature enough to handle a situation well one day, he or she might not have the consistency or control necessary to act in the same mature manner the next day. Maturity does gain in strength with practice, so naturally self-advocacy will gain in strength with practice.

How can self-advocacy be practiced in small, yet meaningful ways? Here are some suggested options for teachers and parents engaged in teaching self-advocacy.

- Let the child identify what they need for the day (materials, books, etc. for the schoolchild).

- Let the child tell you what the daily school assignments are.

- Guide the student to ask questions before you identify the question for him or her, and refrain from giving the answer so quickly that he or she does not need to be engaged.

- When the student does ask for help, give the help without commentary. Students who are struggling with executive function already know that they make it difficult for teachers and parents, and are extremely sensitive to criticism.

- Try to strike a balance between being too enthusiastic with your praise or too directive with your criticism.

We can try so hard not to criticize that we may fall into the trap of excessive praise and encouragement. This does not work well in most situations—a lesson I learned one day when I was working with a college student. She had struggled through a particularly hard class, and was experiencing some success. I was thrilled for her, got very excited, and was launching into a serious pep rally on her behalf when she said, "Can you dial down the enthusiasm? If you are that excited I have to be kind of understated about it. I want the fun of being excited for myself. So, let's start over and I get to be enthusiastic." I was very pleased at her ability to self-advocate, but I also learned an important lesson that day. It was far more satisfying in the end to hear her tell of her own success and accomplishments. She said it all much better than I could have, and it meant so much more, coming from her. Believing in her own abilities had far-reaching consequences and lasted quite a bit longer than any degree of enthusiasm coming from me or someone else.

School assignments are a daily reminder to students that the teacher is the boss. A typical situation that a middle- or high-school student encounters is one in which they are presented with assignments that have explicit and specific instructions for completing the assignment, which might include any of the following directions:

1. Write the question in pen and the answer in pencil.

2. Write an answer in complete sentences, restating the question in your answer.

3. Write a paper using an outline, thesis statement, three paragraphs, and a conclusion.

4. Complete this math, exactly the way I showed you, and show all your work.

5. Read the book and fill out the assigned graphic organizer.

There is nothing inherently wrong with assignments and directions like the ones listed here, and there is nothing wrong with teaching a student how to approach learning from a variety of perspectives. The problem arises when the student is presented with a one-way learning process where only the teacher is allowed input. As teachers, it is sometimes hard to remember that our way of approaching learning might be very different from the approach of the students we teach. (Remember, as teachers we "teach who we are.") The school systems we work for have directives that we must follow, and our own disposition affects us. It is not surprising, then, that students do not consistently relate to our teaching style.

Some teachers are quietly teaching self-advocacy at all times. The assignments from these teachers will be varied, not always addressing only one kind of skill, and provide options from which the student to choose. For example, there might be three different presentation styles allowed and the student can choose from the options: written work, an audio/video or verbal presentation, or an artistic presentation. When students are given choices, they tend to engage more energetically with the assignment. A student reacting to an unwelcome assignment might say, "This is a stupid assignment.

I don't understand what the teacher wants. I can't do this kind of stuff." Given a choice of options, then they will say, "I want to do a verbal presentation! I am really good at talking and it is more fun." The student feels engaged in the choice, is able to identify personal strengths to work with, and is advocating for what he or she can do.

- Our task as teachers is to provide students with ample opportunities for learning about how they learn.
- Self-advocacy and self-responsibility begin with self-awareness.

CHAPTER 4

Preview and Review

Mental Image

- Why are preview and review so important to executive function?

- How does making a mental image of experiences strengthen executive function?

For many years I conducted teacher evaluations in a huge variety of classrooms. I was privileged during those years to observe a range from good teachers to absolutely outstanding teachers providing excellent educational experiences for their students. I started to wonder if there was one element that made a substantial difference between being a good teacher and being an outstanding, brilliant teacher. I started compiling a short list of those qualities that were universal elements for being a great teacher, and on that list I included:

1. If you "teach who you are," then who you are matters a great deal.

2. Content that comes alive through imagination is more "teachable."

3. A happy, trusting teacher–student relationship is vital for the student's learning success.

4. The few teachers who practice preview and review have the most relaxed and engaged students.

So this was a big surprise for me. The first three elements seemed rather obvious, but the element of using preview and review as a teaching tool was an unexpected addition to this very short list of successful teacher "golden rules." I subsequently spent quite a bit of time observing the use of preview and review in classrooms of different age levels and became increasingly impressed by the results.

The teacher, the parent, and the student will each use preview and review somewhat differently. The teacher can start the day or the lesson with a little preview of what is coming, and then, at the end of the day or lesson, review briefly what was covered, and give a preview of what is coming on the next day. I noticed that many teachers gave a preview of the lesson at the beginning and a quick review of the lesson at the end, but very few added the little preview of the next day. Yet, the little preview of tomorrow might be the most important one! The student takes that little preview into sleep, and the next day the content or the lesson is expected. This very small deed has far reaching consequences. A brief preview of the coming day, event, or task provides predictability for the students so that they can know ahead of time what is coming. This serves to ease anxiety, fear, and apprehension about what is coming toward the students from the future. It also prepares the way for the reunion or the remeeting of the event or expectation, so the student experiences it as familiar rather than new or threatening. Another effect of preview is to ease the students so they are able to take their memories calmly into sleep and consolidate them into the long-term memory storage. There will be more about how this works in Chapter 10, but it is important to know that we all need sleep in order to consolidate our memories.

The teacher can also give a preview of the whole course and how the course is structured, so that there is a greater context for the individual lesson previews. The lesson overviews are brief, usually succinct formulations of the material or the expectations of the lesson, and should not take up too much time. The effect on the students, though, can be dramatic. If the students are told what is coming, then, when they arrive at that point in the lesson, it will seem familiar, and often far less threatening. We all tend to fear the unknown, so merely by mentioning what is coming, it is no longer the unknown, but rather an expected and therefore more comfortable experience.

In his recent book, *Brain Bugs*, Dean Buonomano (2011) discusses two aspects of memory and the human mind. "First, knowledge is stored in an associative manner: related concepts are linked to each other. Second, thinking of one concept somehow 'spreads' to other, related concepts, making them more likely to be recalled." He goes on to say, "this unconscious and automatic phenomenon is known as *priming*" (Buonomano 2011, p.20). The brain hears a word, or a series of words, and the next thing that comes to mind is something related to this series. This is the effect of preview. A preview, no matter how brief, will prime the brain and make it more receptive to hearing the content again. Buonomano cites numerous studies and gives examples of how this works, making it very clear that even saying one word in advance prepares the brain to understand differently than it would have without the priming.

I play a game with groups of students that demonstrates the priming principle very well. We stand in a circle, tossing a ball from one person to another. The thrower says a word, and the catcher has to say a completely unrelated word while throwing the ball to the next person. If there are three or more people in the circle, you can get more balls going; just keep the number of balls smaller than the number of players. Several things begin to happen with this game. The students often need time to think, because the word that pops in their head is related to the word just said, so they have to think about the word they will say. By the time this is done, the next ball and the next word are already coming at them, so they have to start a new thinking process. Then another ball is already on the way. It takes a few minutes, but soon you begin almost to ignore what the last person said, and just start thinking of random words of your own. Or you might start responding to other words spoken by other players, making your own words relate to them. The pull to relate your words to words spoken by others is very strong. To avoid this, I have seen students come up with their own pattern of words—for example, all their words relate to a kind of work (wood, saw, lumber, etc.); or all their words start with one letter of the alphabet. The brain is receptive to patterning, so the urge to pattern or to respond to priming is so strong that it takes a full decision to resist it. After playing the game for five or more minutes using the rule of words that are unrelated, we change and start playing that the words have to be related. This is suddenly difficult. The priming has already happened for saying an unrelated word, so a quick shift to saying related words is hard. It does not take long to get back to feeling relaxed about saying related words, though, so that adjustment is quicker. This game is relevant alongside the conversation about flexibility and for shift, which we will come to in Chapter 14.

You can teach students to use preview on their own in several ways. For example, at the beginning of a course, teach the students how to preview the textbook, to become familiar with the overview of content to be covered, and with how the material is presented in the book. If the students are dealing with an assignment, a preview of the work will give them a good idea of how to manage time, and what materials are needed, and make the work seem familiar. The students can preview the assignment guidelines before beginning to write, and create outlines that are based on those guidelines. Students can overview the content of a subject while preparing for a test, keeping a sense of the context in place, which will strengthen their ability to remember the material.

Parents can use preview by each evening preparing for the coming day—putting out the materials needed, helping with the process of packing school materials, preparing school lunches, laying out clothes, etc. There is a great deal of variety in family life, but each family needs to prepare for coming events in a way that is practical for them. It is a good idea to organize events through a family calendar, using any medium that works. Paper calendars can be visual and colourful. Electronic calendars can be shared, and alerts can be set up if needed as reminders of upcoming events. The goal is to make preparation and family organization easy and successful.

Another kind of preview takes place at bedtime when a parent reflects on what happened that day, and tells the child about what is coming up the next day. This is such a simple thing to do, and takes seconds rather than minutes. The younger the child, the more this can and should be a little ritual in the evening before the child goes to sleep. Healthy sleep is important for learning and for memory, and this is one more way to prepare for a good night's sleep. Everyone is helped by getting a good night's sleep, and the little bedtime rituals that make it possible for children to get to sleep can make the difference between too little and enough sleep. Add a short preview of the coming day to the bedtime ritual, and children will wake up in the morning more ready for the day to come. You never get too old for preview; adults usually just call it "preparing." We now also understand previews of all kinds to be a way of priming the brain to make it more receptive to the thoughts, feelings, and events that lie ahead.

> A powerful example of the value of preview came one day from a wonderful little boy named Duncan. I was teaching second grade, it was early in the school year, and it was early in the morning. We had been working for under an hour, and I was in the middle of teaching the day's lesson. Suddenly, there was an ear-splitting, heart-stopping scream in the room. I stopped in mid-sentence and slowly scanned the room to see where this unearthly sound came from and who had made it. Eventually, my eyes settled on Duncan, who was sitting there looking incredibly distressed. I went to him, invited him to join me just outside the classroom door on the deck, and sat down quietly next to him. We sat there for a moment, and then I said, "Can you tell me about it?" "I just had to do that," he said. "Ah," I said, "Can you tell me more?" Then Duncan said that I hadn't told him what was coming that day, and that I had to tell what was coming that day. So I agreed to do this better in the future, and when we came back into the room, he settled quietly down at his desk. From then on, I always told the students the very first thing in the morning what we were going to be doing that day, and I told them that if any changes came up in the course of the day, I would let them know right away. I also started previewing the next day just before the students went home. Duncan was happy with this arrangement, the other students did not seem to mind hearing about the day's schedule in advance, and life continued quite happily in the classroom. The daily schedule was always on the board, but for Duncan the visual schedule did not satisfy him as much as the verbal accounting. I credit Duncan with teaching me a valuable lesson about the value of preview, and have been more mindful and respectful of it ever since.

Review is equally important. Every teacher can review the previous day's material at the beginning of a new day. This will help the students reengage with the content through memory. The teacher can review previous skills, previous projects, previous lessons, and previous ideas in preparation for starting in a new area of schoolwork.

Parents have a multitude of opportunities to practice review. They can review the day at bedtime, review what everyone did that day when the family gathers for the evening meal, can review an event like a sporting event or a social event. Review gives everyone in the family a chance to reflect and build memories, and helps integrate their past experiences into the present.

Students can use review by going back over a chapter in a book, reminding themselves of the section headings, the highlights, or the charts of facts. Students can also go over their planner, or whatever they use to record assignments if they do not use a planner. They can compare how they completed the homework assignment with how they felt about the material in class. This will give them insight into how they were able to retain the material from the lesson. Reviewing material in preparation for a test can take many forms, depending on the age of the students and the subject being studied. There are many ideas and strategies suggested in books on study skills, such as using flashcards, writing outlines, making notes, and recording important information so it can be learned by listening to it again.

All these ideas are useful if you know how to choose the one that is right for you personally. Strategies are not generic and cannot be simply applied without understanding. As you teach students to understand the ingredients, they will become more skilled at choosing the strategy that will work for them, and they will understand why it works. Review is a way of reflecting, and when students study for a test, they can review with a strong organizational component. It is important to teach students how to understand their organizational strengths and weaknesses and identify the strategies that will work best for them. No other strategies really matter if the students can find the right ones for themselves.

Surprising as it may sound, review can be very effective, if not the most effective, if done backwards. Going backwards through the day's events, or a set of facts, or a single lesson, can intensify the understanding of the events and strengthen recall. It is also an effective behavioral intervention for children with Attention Deficit Hyperactivity Disorder (ADHD).

> Tony, for example, was a child with ADHD. As a six-year-old first grader, he was not able to remain in his seat for longer than a few minutes at a time; he moved around the room or moved in his seat nearly non-stop. He blurted out, interrupted frequently, and was often inappropriate with his comments. He was loud, he was bossy, and he had no idea about boundaries. At the same time, he was charming, imaginative, funny, and wanted to please more than anything. He desperately wanted friends; he was smart enough to do all his work, though he was challenged by math. More often than not, if he was at my side, literally standing next to me, he could settle down enough to not cause a disturbance. Tony was a lovable, nearly uncontrollable force in the room. The other children wanted to be friends with him, but he was never able to settle into any game or activity long enough to show how much of a playmate he could be. It did not feel right to always tell him what he should not do, to be always asking him to stop. I tried to find ways to redirect his activity positively in the moment.
>
> Two months in to the school year, I started keeping him for a few minutes after school each day, and after every other student was gone, we talked through the day. "So, Tony, tell me about your day, backwards. What happened at the end of the day?" After he told me the last thing that had happened, we continued to move backwards through the day until we arrived at the morning, and at times even included the time before he got to school. This activity made a huge difference. There were even times during the day when he did something positive, and I could say to him, "Tony, this will be a nice part of our review at the end of the day. I look forward to thinking back on this one!" These moments would always get a big smile out of him, and we were literally previewing our review. This was just one of the positive interventions I provided for Tony, and although it did not cure his ADHD, it did help in the day-to-day management of his behavior.

In current literature on executive functions, preview and review are incorporated in activities called "verbal and nonverbal working memory." As terms, they are not easily or intuitively understood, but they are important nonetheless. Barkley (2010) calls nonverbal working memory "using the mind's eye." He describes it as follows:

> Nonverbal working memory is the first of the four executive functions to develop, right alongside your ability to inhibit the immediate urges to act. It's the capacity to hold information in mind—not through words but through your senses. So this executive function allows you to hold in your head pictures, sounds, tastes, touches, and scents. Because vision is our most important sense for survival, nonverbal working memory largely represents the ability to engage in visual imagery—to "see to yourself" in your mind's eye. A close second in importance is hearing, so we can also "hear to ourselves" using nonverbal working memory. More accurately, we resee past events and rehear past sounds and the things others have said to us. (Barkley 2010, p.72)

Barkley goes on to discuss eight steps of the process for using nonverbal working memory. In my work, I talk about nonverbal working memory as a tool for linking the past, present, and future for the students. Looking back on a previous experience, we reflect on what happened and gather the information together related to the experience or event. Then, we look at that experience in relation to the present and ask, "So, how did that experience work out for you? If you had to do it over again, would you change anything? What would you change? Why would you change it?" Then, looking toward the future, "What new decisions will you make based on this experience and insight?"

An actual conversation using nonverbal working memory is as follows:

"Gavin, how are things going in school?"

"OK, I guess."

"How are you doing in English?"

"I am failing right now."

"Do you know why?"

"Yeah, I think it is because I have missed a bunch of homework assignments, and I didn't hand in my essay on time."

"Let's look at your planner and see which assignments are missing."

"I haven't written anything in my planner."

"Do you have any record of what assignments are missing?"

"Not really."

So it is pretty easy to guess what the source of the homework problem is, but that still does not change or solve the problem. At this point in the conversation, I will have Gavin talk through a class period, asking him to describe where he sits in the classroom, what he does with his books and backpack when he is there, where the teacher is in the room, what he sees when he looks forward in the room, how the lesson proceeds, and how the teacher communicates the homework assignment. We have virtually recreated the sensory experience of the classroom in his mind's eye, and he can safely talk about what it is like for him to be there. He is sharing valuable information with me about how he processes the classroom environment and the specific lesson, about his relationships with the teacher and his classmates, and how he sees the need for recording information (or not). Then it is time for the wonderful question, "So how did that work for you?" Chances are good that at this point Gavin can admit that his system is not working very well, since he does not record his homework anywhere, he relies on his memory to get him through, and his friends are a major source of entertainment and distraction in the classroom. He wants to do better, he sees that failing to hand in his homework is not viable, and he realizes that he will not get into the high school he wants if his grades are so low. The next question for him is, "Gavin, which of these important areas do you want to work on first?" The choice is his, but after our somewhat lengthy conversation, he can see how effective it will be if he has a better assignment recording system, so he asks for help in choosing a new system that will work for him. By choosing just one thing to change, he can feel empowered and he will likely be successful with implementing and maintaining the one change.

The process of recalling and reflecting on previous experiences, measuring those experiences against present realities, and making new decisions for the future uses nonverbal working memory to strengthen executive function skills. In real time, it actually takes only a short moment to reflect on an experience, measure it in relation to present needs, and make a new decision about what you want to do in the future. Although creating a mental image usually happens in a matter of a second or two, it is a valuable exercise to take the time to think through the whole process as Gavin did, and really figure out what might be a good approach to dealing with the decision that needs to be made.

Creating mental pictures is an essential ingredient of nonverbal working memory and is used as part of reflecting, reviewing, and making new choices for the future. We use mental pictures all the time in academic learning. Reading comprehension relies on students being able to make pictures of what they are reading. Writing is dependent on making mental pictures of the story or content. Planning an essay or report is based on a mental picture of what is being written about. Math is connected to mental pictures of math process, the quality of the number, and the number relationships. Mental pictures, verbal and nonverbal working memory are needed for everything, so it is worth spending time to develop these skills.

These "reseeing and rehearing" activities give us orientation in our experiences. The act of organizing our experiences through preview and review is a kind of precursor to planning. Preview and review provide us with the context of our experiences. Creating mental images helps us to make good decisions for the future, based on past experiences. These two activities are, in essence, ordering principles. They give us the possibility to create order out of chaos.

- Preview and review provide context to the student's experiences.

- Preview and review strengthen decision-making.

- Mental images are essential for verbal and nonverbal working memory, and therefore essential for strengthening executive function.

CHAPTER 5

Motivation and Incentive

- What is the difference between motivation and incentive?

- How can motivation and incentive be used to improve executive function?

Students with executive dysfunction or weakness are frequently accused of being lazy and unmotivated. Teachers and parents both describe their frustration with students who do not hand in their homework on time, do not get started on reports in a timely manner, do not put sufficient effort into assignments, do not help around the house, clean up their room, keep their papers organized, do not volunteer information in class, write in their planner, ask for help, respond well to nagging… Maybe this is enough of the irritating and annoying behaviors that parents and teachers so readily criticize. Ultimately, the indictment comes down to a declaration that the student is lazy or unmotivated. In the face of this recrimination, students stand guilty until proven innocent. There is little they can do to defend themselves, except to say that they are not lazy. Yes, the teacher or parent has observed the behaviors listed above, but instead of understanding what is behind the behavior, it is declared negative, bad, and wrong.

Now we come back to that interesting question: if someone comes up to you and declares that you are lazy and unmotivated because you are not performing tasks set and determined by them to their satisfaction, is your first response to try very hard to change your behavior to please that person? A few people might respond positively to a declaration of this kind, but most do not. The far more common response is for the person accused of being lazy either to shut down, or to push back.

A student who is feeling bossed around by all the demands and directives can experience these demands as a kind of bullying. The student who pushes back and fights the demands is trying to preserve his or her autonomy, and will not relinquish free will easily. It can boil down to a serious power play between the student and the adult.

Instead of getting into the power struggle, the name calling, and the rebellion that naturally follow, would it not be better to set the student up in a situation where their natural motivation can guide them? I have often said that I have never met a truly lazy person, and that you have to be unconscious to not be motivated by something. Everyone is motivated by something! It might not be easy to discover what it is, but every person experiences motivation.

Richard Lavoie (2007) wrote about what motivates us. He described six motivational elements as:

- projects
- people
- praise
- prizes
- prestige
- power.

Lavoie gives full descriptions of each of these motivators, but the important insight to emphasize is that every person, young or old, is motivated. So, is it fair to accuse a student of being unmotivated? I have read multiple report cards that state some version of this:

> Joe's performance is satisfactory but certainly not what he is capable of achieving. If he applied himself and tried harder, he would get better grades.

Another one I see frequently is:

> Susie has such great potential, but she doesn't work as hard as she could.

There might also be the comment stating that if the student were motivated, he or she would do better in school. I have not found such comments on report cards to be helpful. Students do not feel supported or understood when they hear comments like these. The parents get frustrated and show how disappointed they are in their child. These types of comments do not set up options for success, they do not inspire the student to do better, but instead they set up an unsatisfying cycle of negativity that is difficult to break.

Motivation is formed by our personality, our inherent way of being, and our temperament. One person is motivated by getting engaged in projects, while another person is only motivated if they are engaged with a partner. One might be motivated by the goal or prize, while another really only wants to hear praise for a job well done. These are natural motivators, and are part of what make each student unique.

Intrinsic motivation cannot easily be changed by simply being told to be motivated by something different. It cannot be easily resisted. Teachers actually cannot touch the motivation of a student. Motivation is private and personal. The student can, however, work with his or her natural motivators, which is essentially the same as working from one's strengths. If the student likes to work toward a goal, or likes having a project to do, then that is always going to be the best motivator for that student. If the student has to do something that is outside their natural motivation range, then teachers can try to find a way to turn it into something that is related to the student's motivation. For example, a student who is motivated by relationships has to complete a big project. The project alone is not interesting or motivating to that student, but as soon as they are allowed to engage with a partner, or engage with the parent during the project, it becomes much more interesting and motivating. Always guide students to work from their natural areas of interest or learning strength.

Motivation is different from incentive. An incentive is usually something that stimulates us and gets us going. It activates our willingness to undertake something. In a school setting, incentives are built into the structure and expectations, and are often consistent across the school. Grades are a form of incentive; rules for behavior and the consequent punishments for breaking a rule are consistent across the school. Rewards come in the form of good grades, awards, and privileges that allow students to participate in sports or activities. An incentive is most effective when it is a positive incentive, but it is common to find the negative incentive in use. Threats of punishments and consequences, for example, are frequently used as incentives. Detentions are handed out in classrooms every day, to give one example of negative incentives. Adults often turn to negative incentives to promote the kind of behavior they want. Teachers and parents tend to turn to the "threat level" version of incentive when they feel particularly powerless, and are desperate to find a way to change the student's behavior. The problem with this kind of punishment incentive is that is based on a power struggle between the child and the adult. Threats of punishment are generally not reduced when the child does not produce the required behavior, but rather the adult tends to up the ante; it usually only gets worse and the threats intensify.

Teachers and parents can get stuck into this cycle way too easily. The first levels of punishment progress to stronger, and ever more severe levels of punishment. Punishments are always initiated as incentives for the child to change his or her behavior. The reason it does not usually work is because the child has to accept a specific punishment as the incentive in order to change his or her behavior or actions. If it is just an "outer" punishment, then it will not bring about the necessary "inner" change.

Punishment and reward are very closely linked, so rewards also work only when the child recognizes and accepts the reward as a personal incentive. A reward that the child does not want is no reward at all, just as a punishment that the child does not recognize is ineffective. Children can develop resistance to rewards by the time they are teenagers. Praise, for example, is fairly liberally handed out to students for the smallest endeavor. Through overuse, praise can lose relevance and meaning. Through overuse, punishment loses relevance and meaning, too.

Now we are in a dilemma—praise and punishment are the two extremes of a paradigm that is ineffective. They do not work. Children have built up a tolerance for both, and do not respond very well to either. Teachers and parents alike find that simply intensifying the praise and punishments does not bring about change.

This is where motivation and incentive play an important role. Instead of controlling the child's behavior through the expectations of teachers and parents, change can come about if the child can be guided to recognize his or her personal motivators and personal incentives. A very young child might not be able to articulate this, but a teenager certainly can. If teenagers are given opportunities to discover their own, personal, intrinsic motivators, then they will have the skill for life. In my experience, the reason this does not happen very often is simply parents' and teachers' fear of potential mistakes. Give a student the chance to try doing an assignment or project, and ask what is motivating them to do it in that particular way. Also ask what the incentives are for them to complete the project. Sometimes, giving the reins to the student will produce a great result, but sometimes it will be a disaster. Taking the short view, this failure is a disaster of huge proportions, and the teacher and/or parent has to rush to figure out a way to fix it. Taking the long view, this failure is an important learning experience that had immediate rather than long-term consequences. Learning sometimes ends in mistakes. So what? If the student learned something about what motivates them through the experience, then that was a lesson well done. If the student understands what motivations and incentives are, then they will always be able to set up their life and work with a balance of motivations, incentives, and requirements.

The challenge here is that most adults have not considered what motivations or incentives are in their own life. There are many tapes running inside adults that are the repeated messages from their own youth. But what does motivate you as an adult? What are incentives in your life? Ask an adult friend if they have ever thought about this, and chances are that they also do not really know. Next time you are moved to offer either punishment or praise to a student, ask yourself what you could do instead that would enable the student to access their own wealth of self-knowledge and let them choose how they want to steer their behavior forward. This does *not* give the student free license to choose not to do the work. Here is a scenario with a 14-year-old boy that expresses how to work with motivation and incentive rather than punishment and reward.

"So, Kyle, I hear you haven't been getting your homework done. Your teachers say you have missed several assignments this week alone. What's going on?"

"Well, I have gotten most of it in."

"But not all—so what is your situation at home in the evenings?"

"Well, when I get home I am really, really tired. And kinda jumpy."

"What do you do about it?"

"I need to exercise. That's the only thing that helps."

"OK, so do you first agree that you have homework you need to get done after school?"

"Yeah, I agree with that."

"OK, so tell me what would be your best scenario for homework?"

"Well, when I get home, I need to exercise, so the first thing I do is that. Then I need to eat something, and then I would be ready to start."

"How long do you need for this?"

"About 30–40 minutes."

"Sure that is enough?"

"Yeah, it is."

"OK, then what would you want to do next?"

"Well, I want to do all my homework next—get it all done before we eat dinner."

"Tell me how you will organize that."

"Well, I would do the hard ones first, then the easy ones at the end."

"That sounds like a workable plan. What if you have to eat dinner before you are finished?"

"That's OK with me if it isn't every night."

"Why do you want to get it done before dinner?"

"So I can do what I want later, like computer games or call my friends."

"Did someone tell you that you could only get on the computer when you were finished with your homework?"

"Kinda. I know my parents don't want me on the computer before I am finished, but I don't want to either because once I start I don't want to have to stop for homework."

"So this plan is your plan for how you want to get your work done?"

"Yeah, I just don't like people telling me what to do, so I just came up with this plan. It works for me."

In this conversation, the motivation and the incentive was set by Kyle. He still has to get his homework done, but if he can say why he wants to do the work in this order, then he will be much more successful. Now, if Kyle does not hand in his homework, we can have this conversation again, only this time I can ask him to tell me what part of his plan worked and what part did not work. I can have him process what is needed for him to get a successful plan in place so he does not get continually criticized because his homework is not handed in.

This approach is not fool-proof. Students like Kyle will get this going for a while and then flop and need to be reminded. He will need to repeat his process, change what did not work and try again. The process of learning is never a straight line from lesson to achievement. Learning requires trial and error, repetition, evaluation, and trying again. Just because Kyle tried and at one point failed does not mean he has a bad system. It does not mean that he is not motivated. It means that he is engaged in a process of learning that includes successes and failures. Every time he fails and tries again, he learns something new about himself. Every time he succeeds, he can feel his confidence grow. He is so much more likely to learn from this kind of educational process than he would from a series of sanctions and punishment.

The role of motivation and incentive changes as the child matures and develops. Students become more conscious of their personal motivation, and they are able to recognize the inherent reward–punishment paradigm lurking within incentives. The older the student, the more he or she needs to be allowed to experience the full gamut of possibilities. This will help them strengthen their own inner motivators and make them less dependent on outer incentives to get them going. An example of this is the student who becomes able to work to a high, personal standard due to inner motivation. This student does not need the threat of a punishment or the promise of a reward to get the work done.

- Motivation is personal and private, and cannot be accessed by anyone other than the individual.

- Incentives are applied from outside the student in the form of rewards and punishments.

- Instead of controlling the child's behavior by means of "outer" expectations, lead them to recognize their "inner" personal motivators and personal incentives.

CHAPTER 6

Analysis and Synthesis

From the Whole to the Parts and from the Parts to the Whole

- How can we teach from the whole to the parts or from the parts to the whole?

- How can students use analysis and synthesis as a learning strength?

Jen is a 15-year-old girl who is having trouble organizing her work. When asked if she likes working from the overview to the detail, or from the detail to the overview, she is clear that she likes to get an overview first. That makes her feel as if she is in control.

Joseph is a 17-year-old boy who hates having a specific overview at the beginning of a project. He has so many ideas and such a lively thought process that he feels constricted and confined by working from an overview first. He will generate enough ideas for ten projects before he will engage in a pruning process.

Both Jen and Joseph are normal students who simply have a very different ways of approaching the organization of their work. Jen responds very well to a structured outline of the work and will work through the assignment systematically. She is secure when she can identify the title and thesis statement, and constructs her paragraphs following the order she set out in the thesis statement. She can think best when she knows where she is going, and has an idea of how she will get there. Jen will not be easily distracted by a new idea, or a new theme. She knows what her goal is and she moves in a systematic way to get there. Jen's approach is to work from the whole to the parts, or through analysis. She likes having the whole picture first, and then she works to identify the parts that make up the whole. She analyzes her theme, identifies the component parts, and constructs her written work accordingly.

Joseph is allergic to the structured outline approach, and can only generate an outline by choosing from his countless ideas. Jen feels secure with the structure, Joseph feels he can breathe only when he can generate many ideas and later identify the ideas salient to the assigned theme. Joseph works from the parts to the whole, or through synthesis. He is very smart, and is able to see the value of each of his ideas. He can talk about his ideas for hours, and he already knows facts and details about each one. His attention easily slides over the ideas, and he can readily point out the importance of each. His challenge is to lay all the parts out, choose the ones he deems most important, and begin constructing his writing by synthesizing or piecing the parts together into a coherent whole. He is challenged by the fact that all his ideas seem great to him. Everything is interesting, and each idea makes him think of another good idea. Joseph has to start letting go of some of the ideas, possibly putting them aside for another day or another assignment. His challenge is to synthesize by making thematic connections and pruning away the resulting unrelated ideas. Compared to Joseph, Jen has to use a similar amount of discipline, but Jen needs to push on through to the end. The overview does not provide the necessary details, and Jen has to work hard to identify the many details and keep them in the right order throughout her work.

While students can often learn both ways, from the whole to the parts or the parts to the whole, one of these approaches will be the student's first choice or preferred way to work. The ideal situation is for the student to be agile enough to engage in both options, depending on the situation. Students will receive assignments that are organized from both directions, so it is important to learn how to manage both styles of learning. The following table shows how this can be done.

Subject	Whole to parts	Parts to whole
Reading	• Scan the material in advance to get an overview of the whole piece. • Look over titles, chapter names, headings. • Read synopsis if available. • Read the whole passage first, then reread for themes and specific details.	• Read specific chapters in the order you find important. • Scan and highlight keywords that you return to later in more detail. • Read sections related to a theme that you have identified as important.
Writing	• Set the title, write an outline with thesis statement, paragraphs in order of importance to theme, and conclusion. • Write the whole paper, go back for editing and review later. • Rewrite, ensuring that there are enough details to support the thesis.	• "Popcorn" your ideas, start sorting them according to related themes, begin writing based on the ideas that emerged. • Identify the thesis that has emerged through the writing. • Sort the writing into paragraphs that are connected, write and rewrite the introduction and conclusion. • Rewrite from the thesis to ensure continuity of the thought process.
Math	• How many ways can we make 12? • Start with the big picture and concept and understand it from as many perspectives as possible. • Move from counting and sequencing to computation.	• $8 + 4 = 12$ • Learn math facts. • Learn theorems and specific formulas.
Organization	• Clarify all the work that needs to be done, set a schedule for doing it, identify time parameters needed for each part of the whole. • Structure the project. • Sequence work from beginning to end. • Clean room by just getting starting and working your way from one end to the next.	• Work on one subject or project at a time. • Work on various parts of the project before putting it all together at the end. • Use a fairly unstructured, somewhat creative approach to putting the work together. • Clean your room in sections—square foot by square foot. • Clean up by sorting type of item—books/papers, clothes, games, etc.

Working from the whole to the parts or from the parts to the whole is not limited to academic work.

Thomas is a 16-year-old student who knows what his learning differences and challenges are. He has known for years, and has been in school environments that have offered excellent accommodations for his learning style. He asks for help because he is disorganized, misses homework assignments, forgets where things are, and is causing everyone around him to stress on his behalf. At first glance, Thomas appears completely relaxed with his way of working. He says, "If I get assignments handed in, it's fine. If I don't get them handed in, it's fine."

When he first said this, I looked at him and just smiled. I suggested that he try that one again, and this time he smiled. Of course it was not fine if he did not get the assignments handed in. His way of avoiding the stress of missing assignments was to avoid the idea that there was anything wrong with not handing them in on time. Instead of addressing this directly, I asked him to empty his book bag onto the table and introduce me to the contents. He hauled up a backpack that weighed approximately 40 pounds, and proceeded to empty a mountain of papers, notebooks, textbooks, pens, pencils, and assorted unidentifiable items onto the table. It took a moment to visually process this mountain, and then I asked him to show me the relevant work from today. He told me it was in there, and probably tucked inside the books from each class. After quite a while, he had reconstructed his day, shown me the relevant papers, and could remember what the assignment was for each.

His problem was not a memory issue—it was simply that when confronted with his backpack, it took on the quality of being a big, giant, overwhelming threat. He could not process the details in his backpack because all he saw was the overview, the whole amount. He also could not hold a visual picture in his mind of the details or single items in his backpack. When he got home at night, his backpack was dumped in a random location, either near the door or in his room, and only for the most pressing reason would he dare to dive into it to retrieve the necessary materials for a homework assignment.

This demonstrated to me that Thomas's dilemma was not simply that he was not organized. It was that he was a learner who felt comfortable with the overview, the whole picture, and had a hard time deconstructing that overview into its component parts. He worked from the whole to the parts, but left out the parts. His analysis, then, did not make it as far as the parts. When he was asked to synthesize it back into a whole, he could not do it because he did not have the parts to put back together.

What could he do in a situation like this? We started by spending the necessary time to take each piece of paper or material in the backpack, consider what it was needed for, determine if it was current, identify a place for it, and label it accordingly. When we were finished, we had a fully labeled archive file, folders for each subject in school, with only the most current papers in each folder, and a trash can full of papers and unnecessary materials. Thomas then had an overview of his backpack that included all the necessary details, possibly for the first time. Over the next weeks, we continued to work on his overview as well as his attention to details, and a remarkable thing happened. He started to get homework handed in on time, he went to teachers to ask for help because he was able to find the necessary papers in his backpack, and he started feeling like he was being seen as smart instead of stupid. When he was able to see the parts, he was able to understand how they fit into the whole. Once he saw the whole, he was comfortable, because that was his strength. Then, from his place of strength, he was able to identify the parts, and the cycle was established. He could engage in analysis and synthesis. He was more balanced, and the final result was that he was more organized.

- Students can be guided to use their natural learning strength of whole to the parts or parts to the whole in a variety of situations.

- Teachers can overcome one-sidedness in their teaching by giving students options and choices in their approach to assignments and projects.

CHAPTER 7
Rhythm and Routine
Practice and Repetition

- How can teachers use rhythm and routine to support executive functions?
- How can students use practice and repetition to strengthen learning?

Rhythm and routine are two ingredients or tools that I pair together because they are closely related in the way we use them to strengthen executive functions. Rhythm and routine can be found at opposite ends of a continuum.

"Rhythm" comes from the Latin word "*rhythmus*," which means "movement in time," and the Greek word "*rhythmos*," meaning "flow." Rhythm can be understood, then, to have the characteristics of movement and flow. Rhythm is like the flow in a stream—it is consistent in that it flows, but it is also always changing. Rhythms are connected to the world of nature—for example, the rhythm of the day, week, month, and year; the rhythm of the seasons; and the rhythm of your breathing or your heartbeat. All these rhythms are recurring, but are never exactly the same.

"Routine" means an unvarying or habitual method or procedure, or your "*modus operandi*," your usual way of doing something. Routine is concrete, identifiable, and repetitive. Routines tend to be exactly the same every time. A routine in the day might consist of doing the same thing at the same time every day, or always doing a certain activity in the same order or sequence.

Practice and repetition are similarly related. We practice sports by running through various exercises and playing games with other teams. We practice music by playing through several pieces or songs. We practice math by doing a group of problems following the same math rule. So practice is related to rhythm in that it is repeatable, but not exactly the same each time. Repetition is repeating the same activity in the same way over and over to get it right. In sports one might engage in the same exercise to develop a specific skill, or to strengthen both muscles and muscle memory. In music it might involve playing a specific scale exactly the same way, over and over so it becomes automatic. In math it might be repeating the multiplication tables so often that you have memorized the answers. There is little variation in repetition, as there is little variation in routine.

What combination of practice and repetition, or rhythm and routine, works well for you? If getting your homework done just anytime in the evening is not working for you, try routinizing your homework schedule and see if that helps bring the necessary structure. Instead of leaving it to chance that you will find the time and energy to get it done, set the time and then structure the homework to fit into the allotted time. If you do find the time, but get distracted while you are working and keep jumping from one topic to another, set the order of the work you will do and check it off as you get it done. If you are going to turn your homework schedule into a routine, do not change it every day. Get into a schedule, a routine, and stick with it. Even if you find a homework routine helpful, you can still change the place you study, changing rooms or changing positions to keep your brain activated and focused. This can add a little rhythm to the routine, and offers the best of both options.

If you need to practice your musical instrument, but keep messing up on one specific part of the music, you go back and repeat the part you keep messing up. Repeat it and repeat it and repeat it. This is where repetition turns into memory. If you get stuck just repeating the same things over and over, and you need to branch out into some creativity, then leave the repetition and start playing for fun. Either way, it is up to you to find the healthy balance that works for you specifically.

The most important thing to find between rhythm and routine or practice and repetition is balance. Any of these modes alone, used to the near exclusion of its opposite, becomes too one-sided. We need to keep the balance between the extremes for the development of healthy executive functions. Imagine a situation where only routine is followed. That individual is driven and unfree. As an extreme example, we recognize elements of compulsive behavior in the totally routinized actions. Conversely, the person who works only with rhythms might appear a little loosely organized, a bit too free, and not always predictable. Weather, for example, follows the rhythm of the seasons, but it is not always predictable or reliable. Fascinating, but sometimes the weather makes us crazy with its sudden changes. Students who can only learn through repetition will often miss the context of what they are learning, or the interrelationships between themes within the material. An example of this might be the student who can only recite the multiplication tables in the way they were initially memorized—through repetition. When asked to solve equations using those math facts in random order, the student might not be able to do it. By contrast, the student who only practices and never repeats the material might not be able to call up important information when needed. Repetition might stick the material in our memory, but not necessarily in such a way that it is easily available for retrieval and use. Practice keeps us interested in learning through variety, but it might not anchor the content well enough in our memory for us to be able to call it up at the right time.

Whenever we work with polarities or opposites in learning, it is important to keep in mind that balance is the goal. Extremes of an activity are very useful, but need to be learned as part of the bigger picture, and then brought into balance with other skills.

- Routines are predictable patterns of behavior that are secure and repeatable. Rhythms are events or behaviors that occur repeatedly, but not exactly the same each time.

- Practice is going over a set of lessons to learn them, repetition is when we repeat the same lessons over and over, exactly the same, in order to memorize them or acquire muscle memory.

CHAPTER 8
Implicit and Explicit

- Teachers use implicit and explicit content in teaching every day.

- How can teachers make implicit and explicit learning more accessible for students?

Implicit and explicit are two ways in which information is available. "Explicit" means that it is an observable sensory experience, or it is content that is clearly expressed. "Implicit" content is expressed indirectly, is not readily experienced by the senses, and is not observable. We approach implicit and explicit information from different perspectives and process these two kinds of information very differently.

Academically, how a student processes implicit and explicit information will affect reading comprehension, the ability to follow written and verbal instructions, and the ability to learn a variety of subjects. Reading comprehension is affected from an early age if the student cannot grasp the implicit as well as the explicit content, and it begins with the explicit information. When we read to the very young child, we use simple naming words linked to a picture. The child's first books are usually picture books, so the words and pictures are explicitly linked in the young reader's mind. The words have a specific meaning and each word becomes a concrete concept through the visual picture. It is a clear, observable, sensory experience. When you say the word "ball" and point directly to a picture of a ball, and maybe even touch a real ball, then the explicit word–object connection is made and the concept of a ball is established in relation to the word.

The *implicit* portion of this learning is that not all balls are exactly that particular size and color. A ball might be red, blue, or green. We quickly assume that the child understands this, and if they are confused we show them more than one ball and reinforce that they all have the same name, "ball." When children pass the phase of pointing to pictures in a book and saying the name, we quickly begin making the assumption that when they see a picture, they are seeing the same thing we are seeing, and have the same sense of what is explicit in the picture. If you observe closely, though, you can already begin to see what the child is picking out and noticing first. You might point to the picture and say "dog," and the child might point to the background of the picture where there is a small speck and say "bird." What is explicit for you is the big dog taking up most of the page. What is explicit for the child is the little bird high in the sky. So how you process the picture and how the child processes the picture produce two very different points of reference, yet they are both explicit for the one looking at the picture.

The next phase is when the child listens to the story that is being read. The reader can inject meaning through the use of their voice, making qualities of the story explicit that might have remained implicit for the young child. A voice that is happy, sad, excited, bored, scary, loving, etc., will create mood and emotions for a story that were only words until that point. Out of the implicit meaning and content, the reader chooses what to make explicit through tone, inflection, and emphasis.

The next phase starts with independent reading, and now the child is dependent on the ability to read the words and not only form the explicit pictures, but grasp the implicit meaning as well. In a story about a boy, a phrase such as "When he heard those words, he looked down and brushed the invisible dust off of his leg" creates an explicit picture of a boy, someone speaking words, and the boy brushing something off his leg. The implicit information is contained in what the words meant to the boy hearing them and to the person speaking them. What could it mean that he brushed something invisible off his leg? Why wasn't it something visible?

Some students will immediately understand the nuance of brushing away something invisible, and others will just wonder why he is doing something that does not need to be done.

Dewey (2005) and Vygotsky (2006) both describe the learning process as one that begins with an external stimulus and becomes an internalized ability. As teachers, we teach the outer, explicit content first and then work to build up an inner, implicit understanding of the information. In other words, learning starts on the outside with the explicit, and is then internalized through the implicit. It is my experience, when working on enhancing executive functions, that the individual needs to make an internal connection to the learning before connecting it to more external skills. This means that the student needs to achieve both an explicit and an implicit understanding of the lesson.

Language plays a large role in social interactions and provides ample opportunity to practice implicit and explicit understanding. Many of the students who struggle with understanding nuances in the language of social interaction might also have executive function challenges. The exact spoken words are usually accompanied by gesture and tone that need to be interpreted. If the student struggles with reading comprehension, then it can also be hard for them to understand the meaning of spoken language. Will gestures and visual cues help? The opposite might be true, too. A student might understand the meaning of language, even be able to understand sarcasm, but not be able to put any of that insight into their own words.

One way to enhance students' ability to discern explicit and implicit is through art. In fact, I think of art and artistic expression as the genius teacher of implicit and explicit expression. Color, form, light, and movement all join through art to express mood, thoughts, action, and setting. At times these are explicitly expressed and at other times implicitly expressed. Colors can be combined, contrasted, and used to enhance or subdue each other. Color can be strengthened or softened through light and shadow. Color always gives us a glimpse into both the explicit expression as well as the implicit color arising like the after-image of a color. Music is the explicit expression of a tone, as well as the implicit experience of the interval between two tones which arises as a sound in itself. In movement, the directionality of space can be explicitly expressed, and the sense of movement and balance gives rise to a feeling of stillness within the movement. There are endless ways to describe how art educates our executive function through relationships between implicit and explicit.

Eisner (2002) lists ten lessons that the arts teach us, including lessons about how to:

- make good judgments about qualitative relationships
- see things from multiple perspectives
- problem solve
- use implicit expression
- express through art what cannot be said in words.

There are many ways to learn, to perceive the world around us, and to share our knowledge with others. Art allows us to expand our horizons of knowledge and experience, as well as to express the otherwise inexpressible. Art education alone might be the single most powerful teaching tool we have for educating executive functions.

- "Explicit" denotes an observable sensory experience, or content that is clearly expressed.
- "Implicit" content is expressed indirectly, is not readily experienced by the senses, and is not observable.

PART II

The Executive Functions

In the current research and literature on executive function, there is a wide discrepancy between the terms used and the definitions applied to those terms. The terms are also imbedded within differing paradigms. I have used the following list of functions in education with both children and adults:

- attention
- memory
- organization
- planning
- inhibition and initiative
- flexibility and/or shift
- control of behavior and control of emotion
- goals.

In this next part of the book you will find a description of each of these functions and examples of how the ingredients can be used to enhance, balance, strengthen, or develop each of the functions.

CHAPTER 9
Attention

Preview

Attention lies at the heart of every experience, every day. Attention can also play the most prominent role in our executive function. Important themes related to attention are:

- how we control attention

- active and passive attention

- attention decisions.

Attention is the basis of our waking experiences, and is the very essence of what makes us human. Attention is so central to our consciousness that no moment goes by without us fixing our attention upon something. Attention has also received more attention from researchers, educators, psychologists, and authors than any other aspect of executive functions. Millions of words have been written in the effort to explain this complex, yet remarkably ordinary, experience. In essence, what leads us to the most important insight is a single question: *What do you naturally pay attention to?*

Before you read on, take a moment and write down your answer by listing the first five to ten things that spring to your mind. Record what you are paying attention to right now, in this very moment. After you write it down, put it aside.

As teachers and parents we expend a tremendous amount of effort attempting to direct and control the attention of others.

- "Pay attention!"
- "Are you paying attention?"
- "Please pay attention."
- "May I have your attention, please?"
- "That caught my attention."
- "Are you listening to me?"
- "Why don't you pay attention when I talk to you?"
- "Are you paying attention to what I said?"
- "Focus, please."
- "Hey, pay attention to what you are doing!"
- "Stop doing that!" (Stop paying attention to what you are engaged in doing.)
- "Look at this!" (Pay attention to what I want you to pay attention to.)

Something can be "attention-grabbing;" we accuse others of being "attention-seeking;" and we will identify something that "needs attention."

From the moment a child wakes up in the morning, parents and teachers are attempting to guide and control the child's attention. The younger the child, the more control the parents try to exert over its attention. It becomes frustrating for parents as the child grows older, because their ability to control their child's attention diminishes year after year. Any parent of a teenager understands the aggravation of trying to get their son or daughter to "pay attention" to something specific. It is no surprise that teenagers resist being told what to pay attention to. Actually, it should be no surprise that anyone of any age might resist being told how to use attention. In classrooms, it is no easier to capture the attention of the students. Teachers spend most of every teaching hour trying to make students pay attention to what they are saying or doing. So, for all of us, the attention struggle begins with waking in the morning, and does not end until sleep finally brings peace to the struggle at the end of the day.

We can all fall into the trap of an attention command structure by demanding that children put their attention where we say they should. Try an experiment for yourself—take one day and try to listen to all the different ways you overtly or covertly attempt to direct someone else's attention. If a day is too long, try listening to yourself for an hour, or even 15 minutes. Attention-directing comments are easy to recognize in our interaction with children. In fact, nearly everything we say to a child has an attention-directing element. Tune in and listen to the ways you try to control the attention of other adults, friends, and colleagues. If you have any teenagers in your life, or young adults, does your language change for them? Does the tone you use when talking with various people change? Do you try to get others to listen to you by the way you engage in conversation?

Education is based on directing the child's attention to a specific content, specific actions, and specific interactions. As teachers and parents it is our job to guide, direct, form, channel, structure, and educate the way our children use their attention. It is also our job to do the same for our own attention. Which one is harder? Is it easier to try to change someone else's attention, or to change our own? The answers to this question differ, but if you can answer this honestly to yourself, you will be on the way to understanding the most important factors in attention. Who is in control? Who should be in control?

The real message here is that attention is the ultimate power tool. We can use it to help or hinder; build up or tear down; to guide or command; educate or enforce. Our use of power and control is often unconscious, even automatic. One mother told me her pediatrician advised her to be careful with her daughter, who was a headstrong, active girl. He said, "Don't break this child's will." The mother was asking me what to do, since she needed to educate her daughter, and even protect her from behaviors that could be harmful. This is the dilemma for parents—namely, how are they to guide their child's behavior and attention, while at the same time respecting the child's independent will?

There is no single answer to this question. Naturally, every child is different, with a different set of strengths, weaknesses, challenges, and abilities. But there are some questions every parent or teacher can ask, and the answers might lead them to the needed insight about the child. Ultimately, these are questions each person, regardless of age, can ask of him or herself. The answers can provide an insightful view into what motivates, guides, inspires, and directs each individual's learning process.

First, what do we pay attention to? A partial list might include:

- words

- sounds

- actions

- visual cues

- thoughts and ideas

- feelings

- senses (sight, smell, hearing, touch, temperature, etc.)

- feeling well or feeling ill

- hopes and fears.

The variety in this list gives us insight into how vast our use of attention really is. So the question, "What do you pay attention to?" is the most important one. Now is a good time to review the list you made at the beginning of this chapter. What is on your list? Now that you have thought about it a bit more, is there anything you would add?

What we pay attention to changes after the first impression of a situation. When we enter a new space or a new environment, we immediately notice certain things. Everyone notices different elements, and these differences are crucial to understanding attention. Over the years, I have asked nearly every student to share what they noticed or paid attention to when they first entered my office. I would just write down the list of items, and put it aside. Later, as we discussed other elements of executive function or learning styles, the first "attention list" revealed important information and served as a guide to understanding the student's learning strengths, approaches, and tendencies. One student might say, "I noticed the desk, the table, your computer, the big ball, and the green chairs." Another student might say, "The light and the windows. And the way the light hits that painting. And the walls look light, too." One student said, "Your books. Are they in a certain order? And I noticed your notebook—it doesn't have any lines in it. Where did you get a notebook with blank paper? Am I allowed to use the colored pens? Where did you get them? And why do you have a big ball in your room?"

What can we learn from these comments? The student who noticed the furniture was one who demonstrated learning strengths based on recognizing form, structure, and style. This student wanted to take very structured notes, had legible handwriting, and liked to make note cards when he studied. When we looked at the ingredients list together, this was a student who easily recognized that he wanted to work from the whole to the parts. He needed to have an overview of his theme and the requirements for the assignments, and an idea of where it might lead him. He was comfortable in a relationship that did not shift or change much. He liked consistency and reliability. His attention sought out situations that provided security, and ones in which he could take the initiative, but not too frequently. As a slight tease one day, I asked him if he liked to change the furniture around in his room, and he looked a bit horrified at the mere idea. "Why would you do that?" he asked. "I like it just the way it is. I know where things are and I like having it the same." Predictability and routine were strengths for this student. If he had to learn something, it was better to get it into a predictable format and practice it in a routine way. Rhythms were a bit unnerving for him; he preferred to already know what was going to happen and he really did not mind repeating the same things over and over.

The student who noticed the light was one who had a highly developed strength in relationships, and told me he had very good friends. He was one who noticed the effect of actions and words on others, and he was sensitive to both physical and emotional atmosphere. He could tell if a person was trustworthy (light-filled) or untrustworthy (he described these people as "dark"). This student translated his particular strength into sports and was a central player on his team. His ability to "read" the situation made him a natural leader. He not only liked working from the parts to the whole, building up his thoughts and writing from a collection of ideas, but said he simply could not do it the other way around. He said his teachers allowed him to do it his way, because he always handed in great work and they did not mind how he approached it. His strength was in his friendships, and he described how his friends "had his back" but that he had their backs, too. This student also expressed one of his strengths as being able to enjoy and use metaphor. The more we talked, the more I understood why the first thing he noticed when he came in my office was the quality of light.

The third student had a tremendous knowledge base, was interested in everything, and was able to remember what she learned. She wanted to know "why" about everything, so that she could understand other people better and could discover what would work better for her personally. Her strength showed up in the ability to preview and review. Her natural level of interest in everything was based on her capacity for forming mental pictures. This was why she could remember so many things and why she asked so many questions. She could reconstruct the initial sense impression, so she was able to review, reflect, and imagine herself into the future. She was also one who had good "spatial sense" and her interest was in tumbling and gymnastics. Her natural ability to notice absolutely everything was both her strength and her weakness. As an area of strength, it enabled her to take in a tremendous amount of information and apply it appropriately through her actions. It also was her weakness, because there were times she needed a better filter. When too many experiences were crammed in at once, she would become overwhelmed and it could cause her to edge toward feeling depressed. She understood implicit and explicit perfectly. When we needed to go a little deeper into her organizational skills, we started with her strength by identifying the areas that needed her attention, and then we worked on steering her considerable capacity for attention toward the chosen papers, books, materials, and tasks.

All of these conversations and insights arose from asking the simple question: *What do you naturally pay attention to?*

Active and passive attention

There is an important differentiation to be made between what we "pay" attention to and what "grabs" our attention. What we give our attention to might be the person speaking to us, the activity in the room, what is going on outside the window. This kind of attention is set because we decide to set it, and it changes because we decide to change it. We use this kind of attention all day, in innumerable ways. This is actively engaged attention.

What "grabs" our attention might be a sound, a movement that catches our eye, a smell that suddenly overwhelms us, a song that gets us thinking about a certain event, or a feeling that rises up that we have to deal with. These are all experiences that grab our attention, that happen to us when we are in a passive mode, and these attention-grabbing experiences take over our consciousness. They can be huge experiences or very subtle ones.

We can observe younger children flipping through the various stages of attention. We can engage them in play and activities for a while—and with no warning, something happens that completely shifts their attention. They are suddenly hungry, or they heard or saw or felt something that spurred them to an abrupt shift of focus, and off they go into a new activity. Frequently, if you observe closely, it is possible to tell what caused the sudden shift in attention. The older the child, the more they are able to engage in identifying what they pay attention to and what causes their change of focus. Students around the age of twelve begin to have an easier time talking about their attention in a guided conversation. I might start the conversation by asking them what they pay attention to (active) and what grabs their attention (passive). Often this conversation about the difference in active and passive attention is an exciting revelation for the student.

We eventually begin writing lists of active and passive attention. What we discussed in the very beginning regarding what the student naturally pays attention to might end up shared between the active and the passive list. The student might be naturally able to pay attention both actively and passively, simultaneously. For example, a student might naturally pay attention to what I was saying, as well as noticing the play of light on the wall. This student would be engaged in active listening, and passive noticing at the same time.

Types of attention controls

The next step in understanding attention is to identify strengths and weaknesses in the way the individual uses, processes, and controls attention. The neuro-developmental approach of Levine (2002) is an excellent starting place. I have adapted elements of the neuro-developmental constructs into a questionnaire about attention that I use with the students.

1. Mental energy

- **Alertness:**
  - How alert are you? Do you daydream?
  - Is it easy or hard for you to stay tuned-in?
- **Sleep/wake balance:**
  - What is the balance between sleeping and waking for you?
  - How easy or hard it is for you to fall asleep?
  - How easy or hard is it for you to wake up?
  - Do you fall asleep during the day?
  - How long do you sleep at night?
- **Mental effort:**
  - How is it for you when you try to initiate mental energy for a task?
  - Can you maintain your energy?
  - Can you find the energy to do something you don't feel like doing?

- **Performance consistency:**
  - ⊚ Do you have consistent performance?
  - ⊚ Are your behaviors and work habits predictable and consistent?

2. Attention processing

- **Saliency determination:**
  - ⊚ Can you identify what is important?
  - ⊚ Are you in control of deciding what you are going to give your attention to?
  - ⊚ Can you choose the important theme in a conversation or in writing?
- **Processing in depth and detail:**
  - ⊚ How intense is your focus on the details?
  - ⊚ How easy is it for you to remember details?
  - ⊚ What kinds of details are easiest or hardest for you to remember?
- **Cognitive activation:**
  - ⊚ Can you recognize important information?
  - ⊚ How well do you connect one experience with other experiences?
  - ⊚ How well do you connect the importance of one detail with previous details?
- **Focal maintenance:**
  - ⊚ What is the natural span of your attention?
  - ⊚ What kinds of experiences hold your attention for longer or shorter time?
  - ⊚ Can you focus on important information? How long can you hold your focus?

- **Satisfaction:**
  - ◉ Can you pay attention to something even if it is not that interesting to you?
  - ◉ Do you lose interest quickly if it you do not find it interesting?
  - ◉ Is your concentration dependent on you being interested or satisfied with the experience?

3. *Production or attention activity*

- **Preview:**
  - ◉ Can you look ahead and consider what the outcome might be if you engage in a given activity?
  - ◉ Can you look ahead and get an overview of what is coming?
- **Review:**
  - ◉ Can you reflect on previous experiences and remember what happened?
  - ◉ Can you use your reflection and weigh it against a possible new decision?
  - ◉ Do you alter your decision based on the review of past events?
- **Inhibition:**
  - ◉ Is it easy or hard for you to restrain yourself?
  - ◉ Are you impulsive?
  - ◉ Do you blurt out or talk over others?
  - ◉ Can you restrain your thoughts from jumping all around?
- **Pace:**
  - ◉ Do you have a steady pace when you work?
  - ◉ Do you often go too fast?

- ◉ Do you often go too slow?

- ◉ Can you maintain your chosen speed even if the work becomes more challenging?

- **Self-monitoring:**

  - ◉ Can you self-reflect enough to determine how you are doing?

  - ◉ If you notice a need to change your behavior or your engagement with something, are you able to make the change?

  - ◉ How aware are you of your own actions?

After the student has answered all these questions, I ask them to rate their answers on a scale from strongest to weakest. This is usually the first time a student has thought about how they use their attention in everyday situations. The questions might need to be explained, but pretty quickly students recognize the relevance of the questions and give insightful answers. After they rate the individual questions, I ask them to rate the three attention controls on a scale form, from strongest to weakest. Once the rating is complete, I show them the overall strongest rating, and the overall weakest rating. When I ask the student to say if this rings true, they are generally in agreement that it is true—surprising, but true.

Remembering that one of the ingredients is to identify strengths, affinities, and weaknesses, we record the areas of attention that are strong for each individual. We want to access these insights later, so we will write them down on the worksheet. It is very interesting to see that if we work on these areas for a period of time, and return to the same questions a few months later, the answers are different. People do change and grow, and returning to the same set of questions makes it easier to get a good measure on just how much has changed in the time since the original answers. Actually, you can return to these questions over and over, since we never stop changing and learning.

Jason is a 16-year-old boy who has been diagnosed with ADHD. Depending on the time of day and the situation around him, he can be very alert, fidgety and talkative, or completely tuned-out. When he is alert, he is able to process information quickly and accurately. He will remember homework assignments and be able to reflect on the lessons from that class. He will engage in conversation appropriately, and he willingly participates in the activity of the moment. When he is fidgety and talkative he is in constant motion, he chatters about nonsensical topics, and he avoids sitting in a chair. Any other position works—lying down, hanging over the ball, leaning against the wall—anything to avoid sitting. When he is shut down, he is unaware of what people are saying to him, does not remember his assignments, he stops participating, and he has no idea what just happened. His mental energy level directly impacts his attention processing. If he is awake, then he is fully able to determine what is important and is able to process information in detail. But it is still hard for him to pay attention when he is not interested. That just does not work for him.

Interest is everything! Jason shares this quality with nearly every student I have ever met. If it is not interesting according to his or her personal standards, then there is no way he or she will engage with the material. If a teacher is not interesting, what the teacher has to say will not be heard. Once a student has determined that he or she is not interested in what is happening, it is almost impossible to convince them otherwise.

So what to do with Jason? He needs to have a reason to pay attention. His focus will go to whatever has the strongest pull for him, but in order to understand what that is, we need to dig a little deeper to find out what happens *just before* his attention appears to shut down. Did the teacher say something to him that made him feel ashamed? Is he shutting down to protect himself from criticism and ridicule? Did a friend say or do something that made him feel bad? Is he tired? Is he hungry? Does he need to move? Does he not understand the material and simply stop listening? What causes the shut down?

This conversation might be the most important one you ever have with the student. In my experience, I find that most students do not know how to have this conversation initially, because no one has ever asked them before what led to a specific behavior. No one has ever guided them through that particular process of discovery that leads to insight. They have experienced being reprimanded, disciplined, and chastised for not paying attention, but they have not been asked to describe their personal experience. Asking a student to describe what their experience was just before they started fidgeting generally surprises them. At first they will not be able to answer; they look a bit startled even, and say that they simply do not know. This is an honest answer—they really have no idea.

> "Jason, can you remember anything about what was going on for you just before you got sent out of class?"
>
> "No."
>
> "What was the teacher talking about?"
>
> "Some stupid theorem in geometry. She said we should already know the first part, so she only showed us the second part."
>
> "Did you know what the first part was?"
>
> "No idea. I don't know when she thought we were supposed to have learned it, but I didn't know what she was talking about."
>
> "So what did you do?"
>
> "I was trying to ask my friend. He's the guy who is wicked smart in math, so I figured he could help me."
>
> "Where does he sit in relation to you?"
>
> "Behind me a few seats back."
>
> "What happened next?"
>
> "The teacher started yelling at me to stop disturbing the class."
>
> "What did you do then?"
>
> "I told her I didn't understand and was asking my friend for help."
>
> "What did she say or do then?"
>
> "She told me if I interrupted her again I would be sent to the office."

"What did you say to that?"

"Oh, whatever. She is just a stupid teacher who doesn't get it. I was just mad."

"Did you hear anything she said after that?"

"No, why should I listen to her when she doesn't listen to me?"

So now we have some of the causes stacked up in a domino effect. For whatever reason, Jason was missing the original information. Later we determined he had been absent on the day the first part of the lesson was taught, had not found out what the work was, and therefore did not catch up with the class right after his absence. The next part of the problem was his decision to talk to a friend a few seats away in order to get help. This could not be done very quietly because the other student was too far away. Then the teacher's reaction to his disruption was to name it a punishable offence. She did not notice, and did not ask, why he was talking. Jason tried to explain it to her, but she only wanted to stop him from disturbing, not understand why it was happening. So she stated her threat of punishment which made Jason both ashamed and mad, in equal measure. Any interest he might have had in trying to understand the geometry lesson absolutely vanished at that point. He was angry, so he became fidgety and needed to move. The attention stream he might have had at the beginning of class was completely shut down. He did not hear what the teacher said and he did not notice that the homework was assigned at the end of the class. He was still mad and did not care what she said, anyway.

This whole scenario could have been avoided if the teacher had a few seconds to talk with Jason:

"Jason, talking with your friend is disruptive. What are you talking about?"

"I wasn't here when you taught the first part, so I wanted him to show me."

"Try to follow what I am saying in class, see how much you can figure out and I will help you later with the part you missed."

"OK."

Because Jason is a naturally smart student, this might work well. He is good at math, and she spoke to him as if he was a capable student. Jason listens through the rest of the class and almost has it all figured out by the time he meets with the teacher to make up the part he missed. He feels pretty good about this because he actually likes math—it is kind of like a puzzle and it keeps his attention focused. But this is not what happened, easy as it might have been to do.

In the real story, the teacher threatened Jason with punishment and made him feel like he was an academic deviant. Jason hates being talked to like this, and so when he comes to work on executive function with me, I cannot just tell him to get over it. I can remind him of the work we did on the "ingredients." We spent some time initially talking about all those ingredients, and we discovered some of Jason's strengths and weaknesses. Now we can review the ingredients and use the ones most relevant to his situation in order to help him with the fallout from this confrontation with the math teacher.

- **Relationships**—we know that relationships are very important to Jason, but over time he has learned that not too many adults are trustworthy. He shuts down pretty fast at the first sign of criticism because in his experience a little criticism turns into a lot of criticism really, really fast.

- **Strengths**—his strength is math. He likes puzzles and he likes the fact that in math he can write numbers rather than letters. For some reason he has a really hard time writing letters.

- **Self-advocacy to self-responsibility**—Jason knows what this is, but too often when he shares his need, he is told to stop interrupting the class or to be quiet. So far, self-advocacy has gotten him into more trouble, not less.

- **Preview and review**—Jason has amazing recall at times, but nearly no recall when shut down. He can look ahead and create a very clear picture of what is coming, but makes judgments about it that are not always accurate.

- **Rhythm and routine**—Jason does not take advantage of rhythm or routine very much.

- **Analysis and synthesis**—Jason prefers to work from the parts to the whole. He does not like to be forced to work from an overview first, so he shuts down instead.

In bringing the strengths of his "ingredients" to the issues he faces with executive function, my goal with Jason is to help him understand his experience (comprehend it), make some sense out of it (find the meaning), and identify some effective tools for dealing with it (make it manageable). This is what will give him a coherent experience. With this in mind, our conversation might go something like this:

"Jason, what would you say really happened in math class today?"

"You mean when my stupid teacher got mad at me for trying to understand?"

"Yes, when that happened, and let's not call her by anything except her real name. We will practice being respectful, even if it is hard."

"But why should I respect her when she doesn't respect me?"

"You are only responsible for your behavior and actions. Being mad at her won't change her behavior. It might get you in more trouble, but still won't change her. Let's get back to what really happened in math class, but from the perspective of your experience. That is the important thing here. Is there something else you could have done when you realized that the teacher was talking about something you didn't understand?"

"Well, I guess I could have asked her first for help."

"OK, but say she wasn't in the mood to be interrupted and spoke to you in an irritated voice. What could you have done then?"

"That happens all the time."

"Well, have your responses or reactions been good ones when she is irritated?"

"No, it just makes me mad."

"So, what could you do rather than be mad? Could you take that energy and try to puzzle out the math on your own? Remember, you are really smart; you have a wonderful memory so you can piece together information from a long time ago, and you like to do puzzles. That sounds like a winning combination to me. Maybe you don't need to interrupt the teacher because you might get the idea by just listening to how she teaches the second part of the math problems."

"I guess I could try that."

"Try it once and then let's talk about how it worked for you."

This kind of conversation takes time, but if it happens without judgment or blame, then Jason can understand the overall situation a bit better, think about what he can do to improve the interaction with his teacher, and it might make his overall learning experience more manageable. Jason has ADHD, so he will only be able to go through this process based on one experience at a time. He will not be able to apply strategies like this to multiple experiences simultaneously. It is important to start in an area where he can be successful. I would not suggest trying this in the class he struggles with the most, or the one area where he has a learning disability. Start from his strengths. Build from his strengths. In this case, Jason's strength is math, so working on the relationship with the teacher probably will not negatively impact his math grade—but if he gets mad and shuts down, his grade will be affected for sure!

Attention strategies and attention decisions

Rob's parents are concerned because he seems to get started on his homework, but before too long he is unfocused, distracted, and not using his time effectively. It happens in non-academic areas, too. They ask him to clean his room or help around the house, and not long after he starts the project, distractions and diversions set in. They are not only getting frustrated with him, they are getting seriously worried about what his future holds if he is not able to follow a train of thought or stay focused for any length of time.

I had Rob and his parents talk with me together after our initial conversations about what he was experiencing. We started with Rob describing the whole scenario of his homework in as much detail as possible.

> "I put all my stuff on the desk and get started with the first thing I have to do."

> "How do you choose what to do first?"

> "Well, it is the hardest one because I don't want to be tired when I start it."

> "Great strategy! Then what do you do?"

> "Then I get started, but because it is hard I figure it will take me a long time. That is what is so hard—I get started and before long I am looking up something on the internet, or texting my friends—but I always think I will get right back to work and it is always after one more thing..."

> "If I hear you right, you make one decision to get a specific area of homework completed?"

> "Yes."

> "That might be the problem."

> "What, that I work on one area at a time?"

> "No, the problem is that you make one attention decision, and then stretch it out too long."

The idea of an "attention decision" was a new one for Rob and his parents. They did what most people do, which was make a decision to get something done and then try to keep focused on it until it was finished. Why is this approach not successful? The decision to pay attention to something has a short lifespan. When one attention decision wears out, you need to stop, maybe do something else briefly, and then make a new attention decision. I think attention is like breathing—you breathe in until the in-breath is finished, then you have to breathe out. Or, conversely, you breathe out until there is no more air, and then you breathe in. It would seem crazy to try to continue to breathe out when you have no more air, or to breathe in after your lungs are already full. In the same way, it does not work to keep pushing an attention decision when it is already worn out. Instead, let that attention decision come to an end, take a brief break, and start a new decision. Rob decided to try ten-minute attention decisions, a very brief break, then a new decision. He tried it with a timer, and he had lots of ideas for the breaks. He could get up and move a little, get a drink of water, get something to eat, send one email or text, and get back to work on the next attention decision. He found that short decisions worked for him, and because he gave himself just one thing per break that he could do, the overall time he needed for breaks was very short.

At first, he liked doing it this way:

- 10 minutes work

- 2–3 minutes break

- 10 minutes work

- 2–3 minutes break.

This way he could get 20 minutes of work done in 25 minutes. In the end, this approach worked out better than his previous way of working, when he used to work for about 10 minutes, and then spend the rest of the time trying to focus and stop getting distracted. In his old scenario, he would spend 60 minutes, but only get 10 minutes of work accomplished. In his new approach, he could work for 10–15 minutes at a time, and even with 2–3-minute short breaks, he could still get 40–50 minutes of work done in one hour.

Overall, this approach of using shorter attention decisions more than tripled his output. Eventually, he no longer needed the timer because he knew his own rhythm well enough to take breaks as needed and still get back to his work with focus. He had internalized his attention decisions and could sense when he needed to bring one decision to a close and take a brief break before starting a new one.

This seems like a simple technique, but it worked because it was the only thing I asked Rob to change. He did not need to change any other behavior initially, and by changing this one thing, many things were made different. He had learned a way to make good decisions; he found tools to help him such as the timer; he still got to do the things he wanted by maintaining discipline and only sending one message or text per break; he got his work finished; his relationship with his parents improved because they started seeing him as successful. He gained in all these areas because he learned how to use attention decisions effectively. You really only have to change one thing at a time to achieve excellent, interconnected results.

Review

- Attention is often the least coherent experience the student has.

- Attention becomes *comprehensible* when the student understands that there is a difference between their active and passive attention, and can understand this in relation to personal experience.

- Attention becomes *meaningful* when each student understands how he or she personally applies the various attention controls.

- Attention becomes *manageable* through the use of tools such as attention decisions that are appropriately sized, and are therefore successful.

CHAPTER 10

Memory

Preview

- The main types of memory are short-term memory, active working memory, and long-term memory.

- There are many ways these three types of memories are made, including visual, factual, motor, auditory, sequential, risk, procedural, declarative, episodic, and semantic memory.

- Each student will have areas of learning strength that can be used to establish and reinforce memory.

What image does the word "memory" call up for you? Do you immediately feel what it was like the time when you tried to remember something and failed? Or do you think of the time you tried to remember someone's name and it just was not coming to you? Do you know how your students experience memory?

We remember or call things up from our memory every moment of every day. It is impossible to get through life without using our memory; in fact, we use memory so much we take it completely for granted—that is, until the one moment that we do not remember what we wanted to remember. We feel stress the moment we fail to remember something. Memory is curious in this way, because it is the memory failures that we tend to remember, rather than the memory successes.

A great deal of information is also available about memory. Every student guide on how to study will give "memory tips." There is the psychologist's approach to memory, the neurologist's approach, and the educational approach to memory. The approach I take with students becomes a very personal approach. As the teacher or the parent, you can set up a way of working with memory that is highly individualized by looking at all the options, and basing your choices on the strengths and interests of the student.

In order to get past a student's pattern of (typically negative) reaction to the idea of memory strategies, I approach it from the perspective of imagination. What are we doing with our memory? We are reconstructing sensory impressions: what we heard, what we saw, what we felt, etc. This connects very well with Barkley's (2010) discussion of verbal and nonverbal memory. He calls these two activities "rehearing" and "reseeing." When we utilize nonverbal working memory, we are remembering something that happened in the past, assessing how it worked for us, and making decisions for the future based on that knowledge. In order to do this, we are engaging in a mental process that includes imagination and the forming of mental pictures or images. When a student has a "leaky memory" and has difficulty remembering information, I find that it is often related to information that has no accompanying mental picture.

Just imagine...

The more information that can be learned through imagination, the better it will be remembered. Why does it work this way? Recent brain research has taken an incredibly interesting turn toward understanding what we remember and why. Doidge (2007) describes several studies that taught two groups the same physical skill (such as playing the piano). The one group practiced on an actual physical piano, and the second group practiced mentally, purely with mental pictures, or their imagination. Both groups were successful learning the physical activity; in fact, the group that practiced mentally needed only a short time of physical practice to be as good as the group who had practiced physically the entire time.

This kind of mental practice is very effective when applied to studies or learning anything that requires memorization. We can learn from the mental activity of imagination as much as we can learn from the physical activity of actually doing the action. This is good news for students who are confronted with a huge academic memory burden. It means that by bringing up facts in their memory as imaginations and mental pictures, their memories become stronger and more efficient.

Imagination is a powerful learning tool, and serves as memory's greatest support. A student who is trying to learn history might be mired down in facts and events that are fairly meaningless. The first thing to do is recreate the history from a full "sensory palette." Where is this story or historical event taking place? What season is it? What would the people see, smell, feel because of the environment? What were they wearing? What can you imagine they were feeling? How did they move from one place to another? Bring up images of as many sensory experiences as possible to first create a more living imagination of the situation. Allow the student to feel some personal connection to the subject. Act out scenes as you imagine them. Draw pictures of what you are seeing in your imagination. Then gradually move from these imaginations to the more cognition-based understanding of these events. Any student who has actively and imaginatively engaged with the subject will be far more likely to understand its meaning and relevance. This naturally results in heightened memory for the factual, scholarly content.

Imagination that is linked to the sensory palette forms memory "hooks," so when students think back and try to reconstruct facts from memory, the experiences that came about through imaginations "snag" their memory and remind them of what they know. Remembering is a form of reconstruction, to "remember" it back into a whole again. The parts are there in the memory, lots of parts! But they need to be re-constructed or "re-membered" in order to be useful.

Types of memory

Imagination is only one way that memory can be enhanced. There are other ways that memories are formed, and there are different levels of memory. We know of these types of memory from experience, but no two people use memory in exactly the same way, and no two people have exactly the same memories.

We use short-term memory, active working memory, and long-term memory all the time, every moment of every day, and usually simultaneously. They work somewhat differently and each kind of memory has a specific function.

- **Short-term memory:**
  - responds to attention that makes a quick exposure and we quickly process the information to determine if it is important
  - organizes or recodes the information and changes, shortens or condenses it
  - processes information by filtering, sifting and sorting to prepare it for possible retention
  - assesses if information is new or novel, so that we can pay more attention to it
  - determines what it means, and considers if it is important or interesting
  - discards about 99 percent of the information we take in as short-term memory.

- **Active working memory:**
  - holds information in your memory while you are working on it
  - has a general capacity of about seven items
  - connects the short-term and long-term memory, enabling us to remember a question while thinking of an answer
  - holds information in the mind while taking in additional information

- makes it possible to alternate quickly between two trains of thought at a time, since it is impossible to actually process two trains of thought simultaneously

- allows us to hold onto information long enough to decide either to store it in long-term memory or to discard it

- is the "worker bee" of our memory—always busy, always working hard, always needed.

- **Long-term memory:**

  - is the "hard drive" of our memory, where we store consolidated memories and facts

  - provides limitless storage, so that we can file and access information.

These are the three storage systems of memory, but there are very different kinds of memory stored in our short-term memory, active working memory, and long-term memory. How the student remembers is the key to his or her learning process. Each student needs the opportunity to come to insight regarding their personal best, or most efficient, memory system.

Memory has numerous doorways or starting points. How these are experienced differs from individual to individual, but the main types of memory include:

- visual memory—remembering what we see

- factual memory—remembering facts

- motor memory—remembering through action and doing

- auditory memory—remembering because we heard it

- sequential memory—remembering the order of things, such as the order of a math process

- risk memory—memory for risks and consequences of behavior

- procedural memory—an unconscious storage of knowledge about how to do something implicit; skills storage that comes from practice and repetition

- declarative memory—the type of memory that we use to store information we need for speaking and writing; the memory we use when memorizing

- episodic memory—remembering details of where and when an event happened

- semantic memory—remembering words and their meanings; math rules; grammar.

It is obvious from this long list of memory types that there are plenty of options for memory development and learning. When a student experiences one form of memory as too challenging, there will always be another type of memory that can be used instead. Work from your student's strengths, and use the area of strength to build up an area that is less accessible or less developed.

The memory strategies that work best for an individual compliment his or her personal learning strengths. No one strategy will be successful for all kinds of learning, or all kinds of learners, but it is possible to find a memory strategy that seems to work best in the given situation and get started with that. This is another opportunity to start from individual strengths, and start by answering these simple questions:

- Do you remember best once you have *seen* something? Do you prefer to remember through visualizing?

- Do you remember best if you *hear* the information?

- Do you remember best if you *do* something to help you remember, such as moving, writing, drawing, etc.?

- Do you remember best when you study or work on it with someone else?

Talk these strategies through with your student, because it cannot be assumed they will automatically know the answers to these questions. Frequently, you will find this is the first time the student has ever thought about memory.

Some typical or more traditional memory aids to consider are the following:

1. Rehearse:
   a. self-talk
   b. sub-vocalization
   c. read, write, whisper
   d. trace, write, recall.
2. Categorize and classify.
3. Connect to prior knowledge—make associations.
4. Visualize—draw, sketch, diagram.
5. Take notes, make lists, highlight.
6. Repeat.
7. Paraphrase.
8. Chunk—create word networks.
9. Use flashcards.
10. Use mnemonics—a way of "remembering."
11. Create a song.
12. Use drama.

Of these memory strategies, choose the one or ones that work with your student's learning style or learning strength. The strategy your student chooses will hold the memory in short-term or working memory storage until he or she decides if the memory needs to be consolidated and sent to long-term memory storage.

Consolidation brings many memories together so that they can be stored and retrieved—retrieval being an essential aspect of using memory. Since consolidation happens at night during sleep, it is essential to give our students time to secure their memory before we start making demands upon their retrieval systems. This is the main reason last-minute cramming for a test does not produce perfect results. Last-minute learning works only if the student can hold the information sufficiently in active working memory, if there is not enough time to go through the consolidation process. Many students think they can succeed in holding a great deal of information in working memory, but, in reality, very few are really good at this type of memory storage. Memory moves in two directions. We need good delivery systems for getting the memories into one of the storage levels and eventually into long-term memory. We also need good retrieval systems for getting the memory back out when it is needed. A student might be very good at getting the memory into storage, but not as successful getting it back out. These students typically do not do as well on exams. Conversely, a student might be very good at retrieving information, but getting the information into storage might be more challenging. This student likely works very hard to learn and remember the information, but then successfully retrieves it when needed and does well on exams.

Whether the student is trying to deliver the memory into a storage system, or retrieve the memory when it needed, it is possible to use the ingredients (see Part I) for both types of memory support.

- **Relationship:**
  - ◉ Work together with others when trying to study or remember a great deal of information.
  - ◉ Anchor information through the "relationship stories" in the material—this is especially useful when trying to remember facts in history.
  - ◉ The personal relationship matters, so pay attention to who you are learning with and who you are learning from.
  - ◉ If there is a power imbalance in the relationship, memory will be impacted—this is especially apparent in the power imbalances that appear between teacher and student.

- **Strengths and weaknesses:**
  - ◉ Recognize your learning strengths and weaknesses.
  - ◉ Always start from your memory strengths first.

- **Self-advocacy to self-responsibility:**
  - ◉ Communicate your learning style and your learning needs.

- Ask for support based on your personal needs.
- Accept responsibility for your memories—no one else can hold your memories for you.

- **Review and preview: mental images:**
  - Use review as much as possible when consolidating memory.
  - Use preview and look ahead to get an overview of what needs to be held in memory.
  - Create imaginative, vibrant, mental images to support memorization of all kinds.

- **Motivation and incentive:**
  - What is your motivation for doing the work to remember this material?
  - What is your incentive for doing this work?
  - Is it enough to get you motivated and actively working?

- **Analysis and synthesis:**
  - Do you prefer to keep the overview in mind?
  - Do you prefer to chunk the parts and gradually create the overview?

- **Rhythm and routine: practice and repetition:**
  - Learning that utilizes rhythm anchors information in "rhythmic memory."
  - Set up a repeatable study time.
  - Repetition and practice are your friends when memorizing or strengthening your memory.

- **Implicit and explicit:**
  - Do you understand the subtleties of what you are learning?
  - Do you need to make something explicit in order to learn it?

By going through these questions, the student will come to understand memory better, and will be more able to identify a working process that makes establishing reliable memory much easier. Applying the ingredients to this aspect of executive function will make memory creation, storage and retrieval more successful.

Review

- Use imagination as a powerful tool to strengthen memory.

- Build strong mental images, and actively use preview and review to help establish and consolidate memory.

- Link memories as much as possible to sensory experience to "hook" the experiences in memory.

CHAPTER 11

Organization

Preview

Organization can be differentiated into three distinct areas that organize:

- thoughts and ideas
- feelings and emotions
- activity and responsibilities.

- "My students say they completed the homework, but they don't hand it in, even though there is a consistent place in the classroom to put homework."

- "I hand out clear lesson outlines, and they get stuffed into the backpacks. Are they ever found again?"

- "My son has terrible organization! His room is such a mess we should put a danger sign on his door!"

- "My daughter never remembers where she put things. Her desk isn't very messy, but she seems so forgetful."

- "Why is his backpack always such a disaster? There is no way he can find anything in that heap of papers!"

- "My daughter gets her work done, then doesn't remember to get it into her backpack! When she does get it into her schoolbag, she forgets to hand it to the teacher, so her grades are not very good."

Concerns about organization usually come with lots of exclamation marks. Teachers and parents clearly have been challenged for some time about the issue of organization and have tried numerous ways to solve the problem before they ask for help. Students are also frustrated about organization, because everyone around them is frustrated about their organization and they don't know what to do about it.

Parents bear the brunt of the disorganized student. Teachers notice when a student is disorganized, and there are some good teachers who reach out to the student and try to help. I have heard quite a few reports of teachers who say the equivalent of, "I gave you the assignment in an organized system. Now it is up to you to do the work and follow through with the assignment." Following this kind of statement, the teacher is justified in simply giving a bad grade if the student is not able to maintain the organization system handed to him or her. The experience of the parent is that they have to stay engaged with their son or daughter during the search for a way to make organization successful, whereas the teacher is generally only held responsible for providing an initial system and then simply grading the student on subsequent performance. As a teacher, I know that there are not enough hours in the day to go through a highly personalized process with each student. The parent has a finite number of children that need their help. From a purely numbers-based perspective, the onus for private help will fall on the parents' shoulders. But from the parents' experience, I also know that it is not easy to help a student with organization.

Teachers remain responsible for presenting material in an organized, transparent fashion, though, all too often, students come in with papers and assignments from teachers that are so confusing, complicated, and multi-paged that it takes high-level organization skills just to understand what is being asked. The parent then has to step in, work on deciphering and simplifying, and try to make the approach to organization a bit more manageable. This is what happens in a perfect world. In the world most of us live in, the parents might not be available, or might have organizational challenges too; or the parents and the student have agreed that the parents should stay a bit further away. So the student is left with the option of turning to a friend, a mentor, a coach—or, in the last resort, going back to the teacher for help and clarification. This is how organization plays out, based on the reality of the students' relationships, but it is still a challenge to respond appropriately to the expectations coming at the student from the outside.

The student's organization or disorganization is most frequently understood as orientation in space, which provides us with such a basic sense of security that it is hard to imagine what it would be like without that automatic orientation. Organization in space effectively creates order out of chaos, providing the student with a different option for engaging in life. I think this is the real reason why parents are so concerned when their student appears incapable of organizing. It is important for the parent to know if the inability to organize is a "global disability" for their child, or is there an area in which he or she does have successful organization? Can their student be organized some of the time, but just not all of the time? Can they be organized in some areas but not in all areas? Is the disorganization in their thoughts, as well as physically in space? What is the age of the student, and are the parents' expectations realistic to the child's developmental stage?

If I know in advance of a session with a student that the parent is concerned about organization of school materials, I might start the first session with the student by asking them to empty the entire contents of their backpack on the table. This can be a remarkable sight, and it often impresses the student, who did not realize just how much had accumulated in that one small space. It is pretty typical to hear the student first declare that it looks worse than it really is and that they know where everything is. Rather than challenge that statement, we just start going through papers, notebooks, binders, books, etc., one item at a time. As soon as I start asking for something specific, such as the papers from a history class, it becomes apparent that the student does not have such a clear overview as at first thought. So we start with overview, and understand the student's relationship to "whole to the parts and parts to the whole." How do they see a possible way to organize history papers? What are the teacher's expectations? What is a method they think might work? Is the student's method compatible with the teacher's method of organization?

We sort by past, present, and future, too. Which are the items that are past work? If previous work is not currently needed, then it goes into an archive file. Which are the present items? They need to go into a current work folder or binder. What is needed for the whole course, or is work that is still to come? Those papers need to be either at the front of the current folder, or very near it and easily accessible. So the process of sorting like this leads to organization by past, present, and future, which in turn leads to a spatial decision of what materials need to be close, closer, and closest to the student. The archive folder needs to be close enough to access when it is time for an exam or course review. The future folder needs to be closer because it has the overview of the course and course procedures in it, as well as the future themes of study. The present folder has to be closest since that is the current responsibility of the student.

The idea of past, present, and future, or close, closer, closest, is an organizational system that can be applied to a number of areas of a student's life. It can be applied to organizing sports equipment, clothing, and books, video games, and music.

> Claudia describes herself as pretty organized. She can find what she needs in her binder and backpack, but it takes too much time when she is looking for homework. This resulted in her not handing in several assignments, and it has affected her grade negatively. I took her description that she is well organized at face value initially, and began asking questions to find out more details.
>
> "Claudia, can you describe your backpack and binder to me?"
>
> "Well, I have a binder for every class and I keep the binders I need that day in my backpack. We have 'A' days and 'B' days, so I need different sets of binders each day."
>
> "Where is your backpack during the day?"
>
> "I have to carry it with me to each class since my locker is too far away for me to get there between every class."

"OK, so describe a class for me and describe how papers move in the course of the class."

"Well, in some classes teachers hand out the papers in the beginning and we are supposed to take notes on them, and other teachers only hand out papers at the end because it is our homework."

"Now describe what happens to the paper once it is in your hand."

"I put it in the binder for that class."

"Do you put them into the holes by opening your binder?"

"No, that is too much of a hassle and not all the papers have holes anyway. So I just put it in my binder and hope I can find it again."

"What do you do with your homework?"

"Same thing, I just put it in my binder. But that is when I can't always find it easily, so it doesn't get handed in."

"What is the most important thing for you? What are you held most accountable for?"

"My homework."

"So, if you got a colorful file with a sleeve in it, could it become a dedicated 'homework only' folder? Could you simply put homework papers in there, complete them and put them back in your folder?"

"That sounds OK. I could do that."

"Then don't worry about the rest of your papers. The idea of organizing the whole binder might be too overwhelming, so if you keep your focus just on the homework, you won't be graded down for not handing it in."

This turned out to be a good solution for Claudia. She is a good student, but the idea of keeping all her papers organized in all her binders all of the time was just too much. So, focusing on her homework as a single item to organize could be a successful solution to the problem. Later, if she chooses to extend the newly successful organization to other areas, she can still do that.

Overall organizational disarray cannot be fixed by a single strategy, and it does not stop and start quickly. There is an inner organization related to a person's sense of organization, and an outer organization, related to a person's organizational ability. I find that if a student can understand his or her inner sense of organization, finding a system to implement better outer organizational strategies becomes more achievable. Teachers can help this process by streamlining the organization for their classes as much as possible. If teachers hand out papers, they should be clearly written, dated, labeled, and have the relevant holes punched in case they are intended for the students' binders. This level of organization from the teacher will not be sufficient for all students, but for students like Claudia it might make all the difference.

Inner organization

Each student is a different kind of learner, and has a different organizational need. What are possible ways to articulate an inner sense of organization? Organizational systems could include ones that are:

- alphabetical
- color coded
- in order of most recent use
- thematic
- based on visual aesthetics
- based on feeling (touch)
- based on feeling (emotions)
- according to size
- related to meaning or memories
- based on spatial relationships.

These inner organizers make it clearer why it is important to understand the inner sense of organization before applying organizational strategies. For example, if the individual is organizing by theme and is told to organize alphabetically instead, it will cause stress and even more disorder. If the thematic organizer is allowed to organize by theme, the result might be wonderful. This is the main reason why it is so difficult to help someone else to organize their materials. If the person is told to organize in a certain way, it is the same as trying to change the person from the outside, rather than allowing the person to change from the inside through genuine, personal insight.

It is not only children and teenagers who have difficulty with organization. The kind of organization that you had as a child often continues into adulthood. One adult described his space as messy, but told me it was hard to change. I asked why he kept his space in that particular kind of organization. He said:

> "If I can see it, I know it is there. I can't recognize things when they are all stacked on a shelf, or if clothes are folded up. If someone else moves my stuff around I have no chance of finding it—it's gone. So rearranging furniture is a nightmare scenario for me. Why would someone do that? I see my place all messy and I am ashamed, embarrassed, and even disgusted, but the feeling doesn't make me want to change. No changes. I don't like changes."

> "What would ever prompt you to clean up your space?"

> "It is too touchy a subject. I can't talk about it. I was forced to clean my room as a kid. I wasn't allowed to go out to play or get my allowance until I cleaned it. I hated it and still hate it. I am not sure it helped me. I am not sure it didn't. I just hate to clean. That's all. I don't think there is anything that will ever change that. And sometimes it's just too big a job, too complex, and I don't have the confidence that I will get finished."

The starting point for any hope of changing the way this person feels about organizing space is the ability to identify one's personal feelings, ideas, and opinions about it. This person also provides a good example of the fact that we cannot change other people through force. If this were a teenager with a messy room, a team effort at cleaning it would reveal insights into what kind of spatial orientation the teenager has. Looking back at the list of inner organizers, which one, or ones, is he or she using? Could he or she be encouraged to use a particular type of organization? Parents often sit with their children in my office and describe how irritating it is to clean their child's room, just to have the child revert back to their own disorganized organization. These situations happen when the parent is trying to make the child organize according the parent's personal inner organizational system, rather than attempting to understand which system their son or daughter has by nature. Work with the child's strengths, rather than against them. Let them discover what works for them, and let them try a few systems before they are held to "the one" that is supposed to work.

When trying to come up with workable solutions, it is sometimes the unexpected idea that ends up making a difference. One family described a whole scenario in which everyone had issues with organization. The mom was always in a situation of organized chaos, the house was in a constant state of disorganization, the daughter liked to organize her own way, which could be described as artistic chaos, and the other family members wanted nothing to do with a conversation about organization. After quite a lengthy conversation about all aspects of the student's organization style and needs, we settled on finding a solution for one problem. What to do with the backpack? After school, the student would come home and the backpack landed in various rooms in different levels of unpacked mess. In the morning, it was nearly impossible to find everything that was needed for the day, consequently papers and homework were often missing and the student was not earning the grades that would otherwise have been possible. What to do? My suggestion was duct tape. Although this was a little unconventional, the mother agreed that a duct-taped square could be created on the kitchen floor, and when the student came home, the backpack would go into that square and nowhere else. We also agreed that nothing else would be allowed in that square—absolutely nothing else. This idea has been suggested to several families and it worked in each situation, for different lengths of time. One family continued doing this for a long time; another tried it for a few weeks and figured out an even better solution for their situation. What mattered in these situations was the sense of being empowered by a possible solution and insight into why it was working for them.

One of the mistakes parents and teachers both make is to think of organization as spatial organization only. Organization is best understood if differentiated into three distinct areas of:

- thoughts and ideas

- feelings and emotions

- activity and responsibilities.

Organization of thoughts and ideas

A child's thinking starts with their immediate environment and experiences. It takes time for the child to develop thoughts and ideas that extend beyond their own direct engagement with the world. A thought or an idea can be about something completely removed from the physical environment in both time and space. The younger the child, the less able they are to have thoughts that are independent from their current surroundings. As a child gets older, having thoughts and ideas separate from the local experience becomes more and more possible. Teachers who are able to adapt their curriculum to meet the progressive stages of a child's developing independence of thought will change their expectations to match the ability of the student.

Teachers have the enormous responsibility to present material to a student in a manner that guides the development of thoughts and ideas in an orderly progression, consistent with the student's maturity and stage of development. For example, when teaching written expression, the very young child will first be able to retell the story. As the stories become more complex, the student is taught how to organize the story content in a graphic organizer, write an outline of the story, then retell the story from the outline. Gradually, they are guided to write their own outline, and from that outline, write their own story. Interestingly, this is the moment in the developmental process when many students have a very difficult experience. It makes sense from a curricular perspective to ask a student to write an outline at this point, but many students cannot do it and begin failing in the writing process.

Why is this so difficult for so many students? Part of the answer lies in the ingredient of "whole to the parts and parts to the whole." If the child has a hard time working with the whole first, then they will not find it easy or possible to write the outline. These students are the ones who can tell you endless details about the story they want to write, and they can even start writing it; but they only get an idea of the whole when they are finished writing. The younger the student, the more this shows up, because it follows the maturing process of the child. The child is first aware of his or her own personal world of ideas and thoughts and only gradually becomes aware of the world of ideas outside their personal experience. So they are not able to have a whole idea that can be put into an outline first, and then written into a series of paragraphs as an essay. These students are then considered difficult students with learning issues. The students who understand the world from the parts to the whole are not necessarily disorganized. If they get labeled as disorganized because they are not able to write an outline before they write the essay, it might take years to change. This is just one example of how organization of thoughts and ideas is based on a developmental picture, and how easy it is for teachers and parents to misinterpret the student's organizational ability.

Organization of feelings and emotions

The young child is fully involved in how the world makes him or her feel. Initially, the young child will have little natural awareness of how others feel, though they might be very responsive, even reactive, to moods around them. The reaction to the mood in the room will be based on how it makes the child feel, even if they are not conscious of this happening. As children get older, they will try to organize the world around them to make themselves feel better. It takes a high level of maturity to be able to change one's personal feelings to accommodate to the world around. This insight makes it clear that if we want to organize the feelings of the student, we need to change their environment.

An example of this links back to the description of the role imagination plays in educating the child from the inside out. Feelings are very connected to sensory input. How something makes the child feel is related to the way the child processes sensory experience. The child is not necessarily in control of the response. So how logical is it to expect a child to have organization in their feelings? One good way to understand what this means is to ask yourself how well *you* organize your feelings in different situations. Are there some situations that are easier for you than others? How old were you before you were in control of organizing your feelings?

The way organization of feelings can be approached is through meaningfulness. If an experience, story, or relationship is meaningful, the student will be much more able to organize their feelings in relation to the event. If it is not meaningful, it will remain the equivalent of a messy room in the feelings of the student. But meaningfulness cannot be imposed from outside the student's experience; it has to arise from within due to a sense of connection to the content or experience. This is hard for some adults to deal with or understand because it limits the amount of control the adult has over the child. It is also hard for adults, because it requires the adult to have personal control over their own feelings in order to be inwardly organized. For some adults, any conversation that involves feelings is uncomfortable, so it is not surprising that these adults will also have a hard time guiding a child through the developmental phases of evolving the organization of feelings.

Organization of activities and responsibilities

Organizing a student's activities and responsibilities is perceived by teachers and parents as being fairly easy. Structures are put into place and a student's activity is guided by the adult through that structure. A classic example of this is the student planner. This structure is given to nearly every student, they are told how to use it, and students are held responsible for their work because it is "in their planner." Teachers feel they are exerting acceptable levels of control over the students, and assume that this will make the students organize and manage their responsibilities.

So, why is the biggest complaint I hear from students related to not being able to, or not wanting to, use the planner? Why are planners such a dismal failure with so many students, and why do they work well for others? Some schools have made the student planner the hall pass, so if the student does not have the planner, they do not get to go anywhere in the building. Students are told to use the planner, but not all teachers give assignments in a "planner-friendly" form. Parents often have a hard time reading or interpreting the planner because the information is incomplete or illegible. The student who does not like planners will not even look at it at home. Again, why is this so often the reaction students have to planners?

In the overall picture of understanding organization from the perspective of thinking, feelings, and actions, it becomes clear that the student needs to be able to manage the activities and responsibilities placed on him or her by teachers, but just writing it down in a planner is not equal to successful management of the task. The adult feels a bit more in control of the situation if a concrete structure is established, such as the planner, but a planner establishes outer control of the student, not inner control *by* the student. A student who is not in control of their organization system has a hard time being truly responsible for the work required through that system.

I have asked many students what they think about their planners and how would they establish a system that might work for them. Here is one example of these conversations.

"I can't stand the planner. I hate it."

"Why?"

"They are stupid."

"Can you be a bit more explicit than that?"

"Well, I don't like the way they are organized. I don't think like that."

"Show me how you would organize it to make it match your way of thinking."

"Well, I don't like the size of the boxes. I would make some of them bigger and take others away. And I don't like the colors; I would want mine to have different colors. And I would change the direction of the text on the side."

"So, are all your suggested changes essentially in the area of graphic design?"

"Well, if it were designed differently, I would be able to stay better organized."

This is fairly typical of the responses. When it comes right down to it, if students had a voice in the design or the way the planner could be used, more students would use them comfortably. Many of the anti-planner comments turn into pro-planner comments after the student has been brought into the conversation about organization and responsibility without being pushed to conform to someone else's system. The bottom line is that planners are about control, and if students feel in control of their own learning environment, they are much more likely to use suggested organizational systems such as planners. If they do not have access to the control panel of their own learning, then planners are an easy target and an easy way to express their unhappiness about being told what to do and how to do it.

All activities and responsibilities are assessed based on who is in control. The more we want the student to develop an organized approach to responsibility, the more we as teachers and parents have to relinquish control of the situation and actually educate the student so that they learn how to be responsible on their own terms. If learning organizational skills can be successful when the student is young, later in life these organizational skills will be a tremendous support to the individual.

Review

Organization is one of the executive functions that benefits from the coherence arising out of the student understanding what they need to do, finding meaning in their work that makes them feel better, and managing the given responsibilities on their own terms.

CHAPTER 12

Planning

Preview

Planning requires skills in:

- time management

- sequencing

- overview of whole and parts

- understanding the relationship of the event and project to the overall situation.

Time management is a challenge for many people, but it can become an enormous problem when there is some level of executive dysfunction in the mix. What is time management, anyway? Do we really manage time, or do we actually manage our behavior in relation to time? Time ticks along at a regular speed; we cannot speed it up or slow it down. We can only decide how to behave within the flow of time, and it is up to us to use our actions in a manner that works with our life.

When I ask students to describe their experience of time, they frequently tell me of the time they waste doing things that are not really important. They describe time spent on games, the computer, texting friends, etc. Time for them is an enemy and they are frequently accused of wasting it.

The idea that time is connected to natural rhythms is generally a new idea for them. I often start the conversation about time management by asking if the student knows the order of the months of the year, or how to tell time by the movement of the sun or moon. They have not thought about the idea that time can be experienced through the movement of the sun and moon, which makes the experience of time visible. We do not use a sundial anymore to measure time, we do not spend many hours of the day outdoors, and few of us notice where the sun is in the sky at any given time of the day. But it is a good idea to teach a child how to understand time in relation to the movement of the sun, to build a sundial, or to watch the movement of the moon and stars at night. It is also good for a child to hear the stories of how ancient peoples tracked time. These stories can include the use of a water clock (*clepsydra*), where time was determined by feeling the movement of water. This was an effective time device that could be used even at night, because by feeling the level of water, the movement of time could be "felt" in the dark. Or the stories could describe the use of an hourglass, where time could be seen visually as the sand ran; or the ticking of a big grandfather clock with its chiming on the quarter hours. Making the movement of time an experiential, visual, or sensory experience makes it more real.

Nicholas Carr (2010) wrote in his book *The Shallows* about the changes in human consciousness brought about by the development and use of the map and the clock. Before the era of common usage of timepieces, people only had nature as a reference point for time. As mechanical timepieces were created and put into general use, their practical relevance grew larger, as the timepiece shrank in size. Eventually, time was fully captured and constrained into hours, minutes, and seconds that could be tracked on a device as small as a wristwatch. References to time became a normal part of everyday language:

- "Just a minute."
- "I will be there in a second."
- "I will see you later."
- "I will be there soon."
- "That will take hours to do."

These all sound very normal to us and we use phrases like this every day—but they are not very explicit or accurate descriptions of exactly how much time will pass before the promised event takes place. We do not use phrases such as, "I will be home as the sun goes down." We do use phrases that relate time to events, such as, "I will be home before dinner."

Young children are not very conscious about time, but their time sense has to change when they go to school. Once a child is in school, a full set of time management demands begins and not all children are developmentally ready for the challenge. For a schoolchild, a precursor to learning about managing the time demands inherent in the average school day would be to learn about the big rhythms in nature in order to give the student a chance to develop a "sense" for time. A child needs to learn about the "big chunks" of time as much as the smaller portions of time, such as day/night, months of the year, days of the week, hours in a day, minutes in an hour, and seconds in a minute. When we ask a child to have an understanding for a ten-minute increment of time, and they have no idea of this bigger picture of time, then ten minutes can feel like a random portion. For the younger child, it is very effective to begin with a sense-filled experience of time (see it, hear it, feel it) and move toward a sense-free experience ("you have five minutes to finish"). The concept of time, separated from sensory experience, is a much more mature stage of consciousness, and a child who does not seem to have a sense of time, will greatly benefit from having a sensory-based experience of time as a foundation.

Although these suggestions sound good, teachers and parents do not usually see how they can be of any practical, immediate use. Showing a child how time can be experienced through the senses is very important, but it might not bring about immediate change, because developing a sense of time takes time. We might start with the big rhythms in nature and eventually bring the sense of time into a small portion of time that can be followed on a clock. So, while we are teaching our school-aged child about these big time rhythms, we are still trying to impart a sense of task-related time. They need task-related or event-related time sense in the classroom, when they are at home, and when they are with friends. Without this time sense, children get into all kinds of trouble. In school, the teachers accuse them of being unfocused, lazy, and disorganized. At home, they are not able to follow directions or respond to a request to get something done in a specific amount of time. With their friends, they lose track of time and might not come home, call home, or finish the project in the allotted time-frame.

There are quite a few tools available to support "time-sense," and they should be used as much as possible. Just remember, these are outer tools that are intended to support the inner sense of time. While you are using the tools, do not forget to continue working on that inner relationship to time.

The following time tools might be useful:

- Timers—measuring a certain amount of time in advance, and setting a timer that will track how much of that time is remaining to be used. This will track time from the whole to the parts.

- Stopwatch—measures each portion of time you have used. At the end, you will see how much you used, or how long a certain activity took you to accomplish. This is time management from the parts to the whole.

- Watch—the simple watch (analog, not digital) helps the child with a visual picture of the passing of time.

- Calendars—these are visual representations of time, giving you an overview of days in relation to one another.

- Visual/pictorial project trackers—making a visual, movable time-line of a project.

Any of these suggestions will work, mainly because they are sensory-based time management options.

Check that the child has the appropriate background information needed for these options. As an example, I was helping a 14-year-old student with a project that needed to be organized over a period of weeks. We were mapping the work schedule out on a monthly calendar and it became apparent that the student did not know the sequence of the months of the year in order. There was no inner picture for what happened in April as compared to what happens in October. This student was not even sure of the significance of December 31st. Sequencing the months of the year in order naturally became the starting point, and after setting up a visual calendar with colors and pictures, planning the time needed for the long project made more sense. The student needed support sequencing the time plan first, before planning the project over a period of time became possible.

Time in relation to past, present, and future

"How was your day at school today?"

"Fine, I guess."

"What did you do today in class?"

"I dunno."

"You don't know what you just did in school?"

"You know, the same as always. I just don't remember."

"Uh, OK, well, what do you have for homework?"

"I don't know."

"Where can you find out? Did you write it in your planner?"

"Maybe, but I don't remember."

"Go get your planner and let's look."

So the child goes off and gets the planner, but there is nothing written down. Now the parent is seriously aggravated—how can a child not know what they did in school just a few hours ago and how can they really have no idea about the homework? Doesn't homework get assigned every day? Shouldn't the child be looking out for it by now, or at least know that they will have to do the homework when they get home? Are they not remembering on purpose? Or are they just saying they don't remember to be annoying? Parents are unhappy, and don't know what to do to get their child to remember something as simple as what they did that day.

The child doesn't see it this way. As far as the child is concerned, there is nothing worth remembering. To remember just means that they have to continue to think about the school day, and if they remember the homework, they will have to do it. That is not what they want, so forgetting is just easier.

Whenever I have a student who is "forgetting" what just happened, I start instead with what they do remember.

> "So, Avery, what did you do today in school?"
>
> "The same old stuff."
>
> "Give me one specific. Start with one detail."
>
> "OK, my math teacher said we were going to have a test tomorrow, but that is dumb because we never have tests on Wednesday, so why is she doing this? She hasn't given us time to even study. The stuff we are learning is all new."

> Now we have several pieces of important information. Avery was paying attention and heard clearly that there will be a test. He wants to do well, but is worried about having enough time to prepare. He knows what material will be covered, but is not familiar enough with it to ask for help outright. All of this information was right there when he first answered, "The same old stuff," but it needed some elaboration and interpretation.
>
> This would be a good time to drop the questioning about what he did that day, and just suggest that he shows what math he is learning and describe what he does know about the material. After he has had a chance to review it like this, he might either simply understand the material better, or he might realize what his questions are. Either way, he has engaged in the learning process on his own, without feeling like he let anyone down.

This process demonstrates one way to use the ingredient of review. In this case, Avery reviewed a detail, rather than give an account of the entire day. Is this his preference? After dealing with the one detail, could he add another detail or two about the day? He might build up to a complete overview this way, but only if he is allowed to approach it from the perspective that holds his interest.

I have shown parents this way of approaching their son or daughter who is reluctant to share, and there are times when they come back asking why it doesn't work for them. In some of these cases, I think it might be because the parent's questions are too loaded down with expectations. The unspoken and unconscious message is that if the child does not give the expected answer, the parent will be disappointed, upset, concerned, angry, ashamed, or irritated. If the child has the sense that answering the question about how the day went will lead to one of these reactions, it is better to say nothing at all. Forgetting at this point sounds like a winning solution!

Those are the more emotionally based triggers. What about the child who has difficulty with short-term or active working memory? These children might not be creating a strong enough mental picture to remember current or recent events. In the classroom the teacher gives an instruction, and the child with weak short-term or active working memory will need to have it repeated. At home, the same child cannot give an account of the school day that has just ended. Now is a good time to try to differentiate between a child who is responding to the emotional charge between the adult and the child, and one who is simply manifesting a weak or leaky memory.

Understanding a child's ability to manage time is based on understanding how they think about the past, how they experience the present, and how they imagine the future. So it is not surprising that we cannot just say to a child you have 30 minutes to complete something and expect that the child will automatically understand how to engage with that time-frame. It is not usually successful if you try to manage a child's experience of time from the outside, but if a child's relationship to time grows in the experience of time, it might work out well.

Using the ingredients to support time management and planning

Relationship

Students are given assignments, tasks, and jobs with time requirements attached. Most teachers and parents assume that practicing time management is an adequate teaching tool. Simply assigning a time-managed task fails more often than it succeeds, because it does not take into account the factors influencing the child that have nothing to do with the assignment or task. How the student feels about the individual assigning the work is of primary importance. The student usually does not see the assignment as completely separated from the person who assigned it. Students will often explain to me that they do not mind doing the work; they just don't like the teacher or the way they have to do it. The student's relationship with the teacher dictates how they engage with the work. This in turn has an effect on their ability to manage their time in relation to the assignment.

"Time flies when you're having fun." Students also lose track of time if they are engaged with an activity of high interest or if they are with friends they enjoy. They will spend far more time on activities they like or choose for themselves than they will on time requirements imposed on them from outside. While this seems like common sense, the important thing to remember here is that a student's sense of time is not objective, and is greatly influenced by the relationships the student has with those who are directing his or her use of time.

Strengths and weaknesses

A student is more likely to use time well if the activity is one that builds from his or her strengths.

> Janice is a high-school student who struggles with time management in all her classes, with one interesting exception. She loves her one elective class that teaches students about the practical aspects of early childhood education. For this class, she plans time to work every evening, she looks ahead and knows what is coming, she happily studies and reviews previous material because she really wants to learn it. She sets up her notes in a color-coded system, and she feels like she always has time to work on this class. She has put all her strengths to use because her natural interest in the material has removed all the hindrances that she experiences in other classes.

Self-advocacy to self-responsibility

A student with chronic issues related to time can be guided to using one or more of the time-management strategies that are listed here or described in great length in other books. The real issue is making it possible for students to experience their strengths and weaknesses in relation to time, and providing options for learning how to make it better for them.

A classic area of need is related to language processing. Often, a child is accused of being slow or lazy because they take so long to process language.

- "Hurry up!"

- "You don't have all day!"

- "You are taking too long."

- "Stop dragging and get your work done."

These children are not taking a long time on purpose. They need more time to process the language, and therefore the response takes longer, and processing the response takes longer, and understanding the content takes longer, etc. Rather than simply being irritated with the student and trying to push them to go faster, it is better to try to help the student to understand how they learn, and help them to advocate for what they need in order to do well. Do they need more time? Do they need to have an explanation? Do they need to type rather than write the assignment by hand in order to get it completed on time? Do they need fewer words overall to process, since processing language takes them longer?

Students who learn enough about how they learn will have a better understanding of how they use time in relation to learning. Self-advocacy specifically links to self-responsibility in how the student understands the time available and manages it accordingly.

Preview and review/Analysis and synthesis

I combined these two ingredients because when a student is planning a project, he or she needs to preview the whole project, and identify the parts or the individual requirements. Then the student needs to get an overview of the time available for the project, and understand how the smaller segments of time can be used. Time management and planning require the student to review the work and get a picture of the whole, then review what is completed in relation to the parts. These two ingredients are in play at all times when a student plans their time, and tracks the progress of the project and time available to accomplish the work.

Motivation and incentive

What motivates the student to use time? What motivates the student to manage time without any outside interventions? As far as possible it is a good idea to let students manage as much of their time as possible, and only step in and teach time-management strategies when needed. Incentives are often a form of reward and/or punishment, so the long-term value of incentives relating to time management is less than the intrinsic motivation of the student. One type of incentive might be the promise of time off to do something the student wants to do, if he or she completes a certain part of the project first. This is fine and can be very effective, but it does not give the student the long-term security of possessing internal motivation to accomplish a task. The process of supporting the student to set up a system and timetable that works for them takes more time initially, but in the end this is how the student will learn to understand the time available and how to use the time effectively.

Rhythm and routine

Working according to a time plan can be structured to give the student the security of a routine. If the student is responsive to routine and experiences routine as a positive strategy, then it will be a successful and effective tool. In this case, set up tasks as routines, and the routine will help manage the time.

If a student responds better to the rhythm of work, it can also be a very effective time-management strategy, because students will always naturally work according to their strengths. A student managing time through rhythm might plan the project to get a lot accomplished at first, take a break and think about things, then come back later to review, readjust, and complete the project. In this approach, during the four weeks available for the project, one student's rhythm might be to get a lot done in the first week, nearly nothing in the second week, and rush toward the finish in the third week, and in the fourth week put in the finishing touches. This is a rhythm of managing time, not a routine, and can be very effective for some students.

Implicit and explicit

Time can be tracked on a clock or a timer, or it can be sensed and felt. Both ways work, but only if the student chooses the one that works best for him or her. It is common to find a student who does one or the other well, but it is rare to meet the student who uses both effectively.

There are some students who choose a style of working that relates to the project. For example, Marsha takes an implicit approach to time when she works on her creative writing essay. She needs to work with the principle of inspiration, and she doesn't come up with ideas on command. Mark takes an explicit approach when doing his physics homework. He knows that he has to use a timer and do his work within a certain time-frame, or he will not complete it. The other danger for Mark is that his attention is a bit jumpy and if he does not set the timer, he will not get any of his assigned work completed. Mark needs to be specific with his time planning or his time will simply vanish.

Review

Engaging with a cohesive sense of past, present and future give us a clear sense of life being:

- understandable because we understand what has happened

- meaningful because it is relevant to what is presently happening

- manageable because we can manage our future behavior based on these insights.

CHAPTER 13

Inhibition and Initiative

Preview

Inhibition and initiative are the stop and start buttons for one's behavior. Learning how to start and stop actions is based on understanding why the actions are wanted and needed. What constitutes initiative? Initiative cannot be controlled from outside; it needs to arise from within the individual. Merely being told to stop or inhibit a behavior will not teach what is needed to understand one's own personal initiative and inhibition.

Inhibition and initiative are the stop and start buttons for our behavior. Understood from the perspective of executive function, *inhibition* is the ability to stop, inhibit, or alter an impulse, behavior, or decision. Inhibition is a mental process that imposes restraint upon a behavior or a feeling. Other words used to describe inhibition are restraint, self-control, or discipline. *Initiative* is the ability to engage with, start, and launch actions that we have decided are needed. Initiative gets you going. You can have initiative as a kind of inner drive to accomplish a task. You can take the initiative and be the one who gets something started. You can suggest an initiative as a way of proposing a new idea. You can see that something needs to be done and you begin to do it. When a person takes big initiatives, we see them as leaders and forward thinkers. When an individual takes small initiatives, we often miss it. But we cannot get through a day without taking numerous initiatives, so initiative is a regular part of life.

However inhibition and initiative are used, they are acts of will. They may not result in outer displays of activity, but they are both actions that cause the individual to engage their will in relation to the decision to start or stop a behavior or action.

Teachers and parents alike find this area of executive function particularly challenging. Some examples of these challenges as described by teachers might be:

- "Your son is not showing much initiative. I told him to get started on his work but he just won't do it. It is as if he is intentionally ignoring me."

- "Your daughter knows that she has to get the paper written, but she is just not doing it. It is due tomorrow and she is just so sluggish about getting started. It is as if she trying to avoid doing the work."

Challenges in this area as described by parents might be:

- "I told you over and over to clean your room and it is still not done. What is the matter with you?"

- "You know that you have homework, why can't you just get started?"

- "Why don't you offer to help your mother out? You can see she is busy and could use the help."

The consistent theme in each of these comments is that the adult is trying to make the child do something the adult has decided is important. While there are plenty of situations in life when this is exactly right, and the child needs to learn how to handle such expectations and demands, it is not the kind of situation to use when teaching a child about inhibition and initiative. Keeping in mind that inhibition and initiative are acts of will, in order to teach them, the child needs to experience him or herself as the driver of that will.

Learning about initiative begins with learning to make good choices. This is not an automatically intuitive area for parents or teachers in most cases. Parents often err on the side of offering too many choices to a child, and teachers can err on the side of offering too few choices. The child is then caught between two extremes, and no one is modeling how to assess what a good choice might be.

We have all either said something like this as parents, or heard other parents say something like it:

- "You can have whatever you want."

- "What do you want for breakfast?"

- "Do you want to go to bed now?"

A young child can be gradually taught how to make decisions about what to eat for breakfast if they can choose between cereal or toast, for example, but if they are told they can have whatever they want, the cognitive burden for assessing the pros and cons of each choice as well as the ultimate consequence of the choice is simply too much. Children intuitively know that they should not be given those kinds of choices, and the fussy reaction is just as often their way of saying they cannot be asked to handle such a plethora of options. In the scenario above, the parent is teaching the child to feel overwhelmed by the activity of taking initiative, and teaching them how not to trust initiative.

Teachers have been known to say things like this:

- "No, you can't do it that way. Follow the instructions on the paper exactly as they are written."

- "In order to get full credit on your test, you have to put your answers in the given format."

- "You will do the math calculation in the way I showed you, any other method will result in a deduction."

So, the teacher determines how students will behave and learn, even if the students know they learn better using a different method. The teacher is effectively teaching the students to ignore what they know about their own learning style, and teaching that taking initiative for their learning will result in reduced grades. Ironically, that same teacher might be the one complaining about a student not taking the initiative to get their work done.

The dilemma boils down to a power tug-of-war. In order to learn how to take initiative, the child or teenager needs to be allowed a developmentally appropriate amount of freedom to engage their will in the activity. In the beginning, I said that an important insight is for the student to "learn who they are." When it comes to learning to take initiative, this insight becomes very important again. If you are just following orders and doing what you are told to do, you are being compliant and obedient—but you are not learning how to organize yourself around an initiative. You are not learning to engage your own will and direct your own actions. Instead of ordering a child to clean up their room, or engage in a project of any kind, you can say instead, "Here is the project. What way or ways can you best get it done? Is there anything you need as support for the project?" Then the child or teenager is allowed to engage his or her own will in the way that makes sense for them, and it does not matter if it makes sense to anyone else. And what if the way they chose fails? Again, I say, "So what?" Failure is not just a problem, but rather an opportunity to learn what did not work, so that next time it can be transformed into a decision that might work better. Giving an option to have personal initiative is a huge gift to a child or teen. It is not a free-for-all option, but rather it is a guided option that teaches him or her about initiative and encourages healthy will development.

Inhibition is similar to initiative. Parents and teachers often overwhelm the child with directives and rules that are intended to teach inhibition, but often fall short of the intended goal.

What we have all heard or said falls into a slightly sharper, more succinct form of communication:

- "NO!"
- "Stop!"
- "Cut that out."
- "Why? Because I said so."

More examples are hardly needed here. We all have that disciplinarian running in our head, trying to get the child's behavior to go along the lines we think are appropriate.

In training sessions with teachers and in workshops for parents, I have often spoken about how to engage with discipline that tries to change the child's behavior. There are two words, of two letters each, that cause more harm than good. No one guesses what these two words are, but as soon as you hear them, it makes perfect sense. The words are "if" and "OK." When we use "if," we are threatening the child and we set the stage for consequences. If the child does not do what they are told to do, then some form of consequence will happen. There are two big problems with this approach. First, when you use "if" and then do not follow through with the stated consequence, then you have diminished or lost your credibility. The second big problem with this approach is that you have continually to up the ante on your threats. The child who is being controlled through the threat of consequences inherent in the word "if" is only learning how to manage their fear, but is learning nothing about managing to stop or inhibit an action.

The word "OK?" is also dangerous because it is frequently used as a question that creates a negotiation. The child is given the option to engage in a debate, but the parent or teacher holds the power. The balance of power is not fair from the beginning, since the child only has the promise of compliance to offer or take away, while the parent or teacher has the control over the child's experience. When an adult says, "OK?" to a child, especially when it is in the tone and mood of a negotiation, there is little hope for the child to learn to inhibit their actions through their own will.

Threats and negotiations do not teach a child how to manage the executive function of inhibition. Granting or denying choices and options alone does not teach initiative. These approaches attempt to teach through the negative, but they are not successful strategies. The basic principles I spoke about at the beginning of the book apply very well in this area of executive function. Keep in mind that the student learns who they are, so it will be much more successful to provide "teachable moments" in which the student/child/teenager can come to a personal insight about what works for them as an individual and receives the tools they need to make changes, adjustments, and decisions. For example, here are some options for setting the student up for success, especially if they are in middle school or older:

- "What approach to this project works best for you?"

- "When is the right time for you to get started? What kind of time-frame do you think this project needs?"

- "Are there any tools you need? Do you need help getting those tools organized?"

Help set up the environment for success, and use this kind of objective involvement as a good example. You care, but you do not need to do the work for them. Also, remember that any teachable moment contains the inherent risk of mistake and/or failure. How we teach our children/students to handle mistakes or failure is an incredibly important part of teaching inhibition or initiative. All children are sensitive to criticism in the face of a mistake, so there is a fine line between acknowledging and correcting a mistake, and harsh criticism. Pretending that a mistake did not happen is not helpful either, because it is not true. Some children seem to be born perfectionists, so allowing them to make mistakes is very hard. For a long time I did not understand why the perfectionist tried to avoid engaging in a project. One day, an adult perfectionist explained it to me by saying that if she knew it would not turn out perfect, she would rather not even start. That made it clearer why she, as her kind of perfectionist, was doing so much less than others, even though she had excellent skills and ideas. For some individuals, making mistakes is too uncomfortable, and therefore not an option as an approach to learning.

Another approach that actively develops initiative is teaching through example. Children, especially young children, imitate our actual actions as well as our attitudes. As they get older, it might not be such active imitation, but they are observing very carefully and can discern if we are consistent in doing what we are asking them to do. There are phrases that capture this, such as, "Practice what you preach," and children are quick to notice when you, as the teacher or parent, are being consistent with your words and actions or not.

There are conscious and unconscious levels of learning inhibition. We teach our young children to avoid dangerous situations like fire, cliffs, and cars in the road. The very young child learns about the world through trying things out and will learn how to inhibit behaviors through trial and error. The young child also fairly quickly learns how to inhibit a behavior that gets a bad reaction, such as smacking the family cat on the face, which results in the cat hissing and scratching so that the child learns not to do it. As the child gets older, he or she has learned to read social situations and reactions from others and will inhibit their behavior if they sense that it is not a good time to engage the other person socially. Inhibition and initiative are both behaviors that develop primarily, though not exclusively, in the context of the world around us. They are easy to observe when they are expressions of social engagement and a response to the requirements of social norms.

Initiative is also related to the maturing process. The very young child is impulsive and spontaneous, which is not the same as taking initiative. In order to be able to take control of one's initiative, there needs to be some level of ability to be conscious of one's decisions. The individual with ADHD can have behaviors that mimic initiative, but are really impulsive, unconscious drives to move and act in the moment. A conscious initiative is rarer for these individuals. Inhibition is also more difficult for the person with ADHD and is a skill that needs to be conscientiously taught.

How does inhibition manifest in everyday life as an expression of executive control? Inhibiting a response, or stopping (cancelling) an intended action or movement happens all the time, more or less consciously. What makes you able to do this? The younger the child, the more unconscious this action is. The older you become, the more you are held accountable for this as a conscious action. You are expected to be able to control your responses to given situations. This is related to the reaction/response mechanism. In any given situation, ask yourself if you are *reacting*, which is usually somewhat unconscious, or *responding*, which you can only do if you are consciously thinking about your response? The ability to inhibit, or stop, an action when you want to cannot be taught through directive alone.

The ingredients can be used to work on inhibition and initiative directly. Here are some examples of approaches for applying the ingredients to develop and/or strengthen inhibition and initiative.

Applying the ingredients to develop inhibition and initiative

Relationship

Through our relationship with the child we provide opportunities for imitation, we lead by example, demonstrating how one responds rather than reacts to others. It is very important that the adult does not expect the child to be more capable of controlling reaction/ response than the adult is. I have seen too many adults expecting the child to be more mature than the adult, and that is not an appropriate or fair situation.

Strengths and weaknesses

Use student strengths as a starting point. There might be an easily identified area of strength that can be used as a basis for teaching initiative, such as learning by doing what is naturally interesting before trying to teach something that is not natural or not interesting. Start with the activities that the student is good at, and from a strong foundation continue to work on areas that are not so strong. Initiative is easier when there is hope of success.

Self-advocacy to self-responsibility

If students know what they need, they are more likely to take initiative and initiate those actions. If a student has been successful with initiative, follow-through becomes more possible and it is easier to inhibit behaviors that do not lead to success. Successful initiatives strengthen a student's confidence and sense of accomplishment. The student is also more likely to develop self-responsibility for those actions he or she has successfully initiated.

Preview and review

If the student reflects on their initiatives, and can learn from their mistakes, it will be easier and easier to inhibit future actions that could lead to a repeat of those mistakes. Inhibition becomes differently relevant when it arises out of review and preview, because it can be seen and experienced in the context of the decisions the student is making.

Motivation and incentive

Inner and outer motivators affect how the student initiates or inhibits behaviors. If the student is inwardly motivated, then he or she can personally choose which behaviors to initiate or inhibit. If the student is outwardly motivated, or told and directed what to do, there are fewer individual choices being made, and therefore there are fewer executive controls being practiced. Inhibiting a behavior through the use of negative incentives or punishments teaches the student about fear of punishment, but does not help them learn how to inhibit behaviors on their own. Initiative cannot be applied or forced from the outside. It has to arise from within the individual, because it has to do with personal volition, personal will. This is an important principle, even when the student seems to have little capacity for the kind of self-control that arises from inhibition. It can be taught in small increments, and learned with small steps.

Analysis and synthesis

Inhibition is the action of the present moment that synthesizes previous experiences, weighs or analyzes the consequences of future actions, and guides the decision in the moment. Inhibition and initiative come together as the student considers the decision from the perspective of the overview before taking action, and considers possible consequences of the decision.

Rhythm and routine: practice and repetition

Practicing little steps of initiative and possibly developing those through rhythm and routine will provide fantastic learning opportunities for strengthening initiative. Success breeds more success. The same is true for inhibiting behaviors; the more it is practiced, the more familiar the student becomes with what it feels like to inhibit an impulse or idea. Again, success generates more success, and the ability to appropriately inhibit actions increases.

Implicit and explicit

Inhibition and initiative work on conscious and unconscious events, as well as what is implicit and explicit in those events. The more consciousness is gained through maturity and experience, the more likely it is that the individual will make conscious decisions based on explicit facts or considerations. The more unconscious the individual is, and this is true for the younger child, the more inhibition and initiative is related to unconscious, implicit understanding of the events.

Review

It is easier for a student to engage in an activity or stop an activity if they:

- understand the options before they decide to act

- recognize how the action affects them or makes them feel

- can see what the right choice for action could be.

CHAPTER 14
Flexibility and/or Shift

Preview

Every individual has some measure of flexibility or rigidity in thinking, in feelings, and in actions. The level of ease or difficulty a student has in shifting from one activity to another, or from one thought to another, or from one feeling to another, affects the way the student makes decisions and the way the student acts.

Not all students have a difficult time with change and/or transitions all the time, but nearly everyone has a hard time "shifting" at least some of the time. We engage our flexibility nearly every minute of the day, so even those who struggle with flexibility will successfully manage change and get through numerous transitions, despite being challenged by some level of rigidity.

Most people consider flexibility good, and rigidity bad. In reality, too much flexibility can mean that you are not able to make a decision and settle on a behavior or action. Too much rigidity can mean that you are unable to try new things and adapt to new situations. As the ultimate goal of working on our executive function is to achieve balance and coherence, how do we find the perfect measure of rigidity and flexibility? How can we comprehend or understand flexibility and rigidity? How is it meaningful or relevant to daily life? What can be done about it or how can it be managed?

Flexibility and/or shift are responses to both inner and outer changes. Some examples of the kinds of changes that require flexibility are:

Outer changes:	Inner changes:
• changes in schedule	• changes or development of ideas
• changes in events	
• changes in expectations	• changes in mood
• changes in rules	• changes in relationships
• changes in venue	• new ideas
• changes in weather/ temperature	• changes in stress levels
• changes in organization.	• changes in wellbeing.

Understanding flexibility from the perspective of inner and outer changes makes it possible to establish important differentiations. No one can be forced to be more flexible, no matter how old or young they are. We can, however, create situations in which the child (or adult) can become more flexible on their own terms. Flexibility is needed in each area of executive function, and the nuances of flexibility can be practiced a bit differently for each area.

Executive function	How is degree of flexibility manifested?	What can be done?
Attention	• Shifts attention too frequently. • Fixes attention too strongly in one place.	• Practice establishing attention decisions more concretely. • Decide in advance what you will pay attention to so you can shift when needed.
Memory	• Gets a picture of events and can't let it go even if it is not right.	• Record events either on video, or by voice recording or journaling. • Compare memories of the event with others.

Organization: space	• Wants to have a set/ rigid organization system.	• Have some items in labeled, predictable places. • Have some places that are general collection spots. • Try different kinds of organization to establish not only the best system, but the right approach for the individual.
Planning: time	• Following timetables is difficult—takes too much or too little time. • Lacks a good sense of how much time an activity needs. • Procrastination—has a hard time getting started. • Goes on too long—has a hard time finding a good stopping place.	• Give plenty of warning before time is up. • Give a visual as well as a spoken warning. • No surprises or changes in schedule, give a fixed time for everything. • Allow for enough time to transition. • Plan out portions of time using a calendar, schedule, list, or pictures. • Use timers and visual clocks to establish an understandable sense of the movement of time.
Initiative and inhibition	• Takes initiative only if it relates to repeated patterns. • Only able to engage on personal terms. • Stops action when it no longer fits inner picture, not because it doesn't fit the outer situation.	• Guide the beginning of a new event. • Engage preview and review so there is structure and context to events: make it possible to see what is coming, and look back and review what just happened so that you know if you want to repeat the behavior or event.
Control of behavior and emotion	• Friends don't follow the rules. • Parents or teachers do the unexpected. • Routinized behavior— rigid ways of doing things. • Emotional volatility— easily hurt. • Can be easily emotionally aroused.	• When stressed, self-talk through the issues, reviewing the entire situation before making a decision. • Prepare for events in advance, so the emotional response is not unexpected. • Choose your battles carefully— not everything can be changed and people are not usually open to being changed by someone else.

Life is full of unexpected surprises. There is no possible way to be prepared for all changes, so a basic ability to change gears is an essential skill for everyone. Flexibility might require us to slow down or speed up, meaning that we might need to shift down to a slower gear at times, while at other times we might need to shift it up and get going a bit quicker. We are not always able to determine the level or speed of engagement in a given situation, which makes flexibility an important life skill. Do we actually know what kind of a "flexibility burden" we place on our children or students each day?

> Roger is a student with ADHD and he also shows some characteristics of Asperger's, which is an autistic spectrum disorder (ASD). He is very bright, but finds any change in his routine distressing. He is willing to be guided through the changes, but it works best if he does not have to make the change quickly or in the moment. For example, if he is told that there will be a different teacher next week for reading, he might ask a few questions, but essentially he is able to adjust to the new teacher. Because he is prepared for the new teacher to be unfamiliar with the routine, he is able to adapt to the small changes in the flow of the lesson. He generally likes the lesson to be organized in the same order every day. If there has to be a change, he handles it better if he is simply told what the change will be at the beginning of the lesson, and he has a moment to make the inner adjustment.
>
> Aaron has language processing challenges, possibly auditory processing disorder, and he has dyslexia. Socially, he manages transitions well and is able to adjust to a new teacher with ease. His language processing challenges make it very hard for him to be cognitively flexible. He sees the words on the page, and he cannot get his brain to recognize them quickly enough, so he cannot respond to the demands of the situation, such as being asked to read a passage during reading class. Part of his challenge is language-based, and he has difficulty with phonological processing. The other part of his challenge is simply that he struggles when he needs to move quickly from one thought to another. He knows he should be able to read the passage in the book, so when he cannot do it fast enough his frustration further inhibits his ability to be flexible and move from one sentence to the other with ease. Aaron can

manage the large transitions of life, and is not too challenged by outer changes, but his flexibility challenges manifest in the area of fluent processing speeds. He needs dedicated, specific instruction in reading and language processing. But the language and literacy instruction has an additional effect, because when we help a child with fluent and flexible use of language, we are also strengthening the executive function of shift and flexibility.

A student might find that moving from the big picture to the details is a challenging shift. Some students describe this as the reason they struggle with written expression. They get one idea for a written assignment, and they are not able to shift it to a new perspective or approach. The student might be able to get the overview and not be able to shift to the various details. Or the student might grasp the details and not be able to synthesize them into an overview. Either way, lack of flexibility in thinking might be the root cause.

There are students with documented executive dysfunction, and such students might have specific difficulty with shift. This might be added to the Individualized Learning Plan (IEP) as a documented learning disability. In such situations, the accommodations are identified and hopefully implemented to support the student. For example, the student might need to hear and see the assignment before he or she is able to process the information. Or the student might need a bit of extra time to start and stop work in class. The student might need time to answer when asked to participate in a lively classroom discussion. Unfortunately, there are times when the teacher does not actually understand executive function well enough, and when such a student is not able to jump in and participate on cue, the teacher assumes the student is behaving in this way on purpose and accuses him or her of being stubborn or disrespectful. When this happens, the student will most often shut down and withdraw, even if withdrawing results in even more accusations being tossed at them. In this situation, the teacher needs more education about executive functions, and the student needs strategies for the situations in which they are asked to do things they are not able to do.

The main issue here is that each of us has some measure of flexibility or rigidity in our thoughts, in our feelings, and in our will. The level of ease or difficulty we have shifting from one activity to another, or from one thought to another, or from one feeling to another affects our decisions and the way we act. Flexibility and shift have to do with movement, so the challenge is to begin or inhibit that movement as needed for the situation. Can the student move from one thought to another, and come back to the original thought as the situation demands? Can the student engage in feelings that are appropriate to the situation, and "dial it down" when the situation changes? Can the student engage in one activity and then shift to another because the situation changed?

- Flexibility in *thinking* requires the student to look at an issue from more than one perspective, to think through the consequences, and to be able or willing to consider more than one option.

- Flexibility in *feeling* makes it possible for the student to see an issue from the other's point of view or have a response rather than a reaction to a situation. When confronted with a challenging emotional situation, the student might try self-talk to make the situation more understandable. The student might also seek conversation with a trusted friend or adult, or try to approach the situation through a story or imagination.

- Flexibility in *actions* can be strengthened through preview and review. The student can look ahead and see where the action will take him or her, and therefore be prepared. Review allows for the needed reflection, so if the student decides to repeat an action or make a new decision, he or she can base that decision on a measured consideration of previous experiences. The decision to act is then in an appropriate context.

Essentially, flexibility and shift allow us to start and stop, speed up and slow down, change directions, change plans, learn from experience, and adapt.

Review

Students need flexibility in order to:

- start and stop, or initiate and inhibit behaviors and attention

- change speed—speed up or slow down appropriate to the situation

- review and preview—learn from experiences and be flexible enough to change behavior and attention accordingly

- be adaptable in variable situations.

CHAPTER 15

Control of Behavior and Control of Emotion

Preview

Control of one's behavior and control of one's emotions can only arise out of a very personal, inner place. Education of any kind needs to arise from inside the individual, through personal volition, coming from personal initiative, based on personal control.

"Self-regulation" and "self-control" are terms often used alongside the terms "control of emotion" and "control of behavior." Of all the executive functions, this one is the most likely to be experienced based on extremes. Both emotions and behavior capture our attention when they reach toward the extremes. Extreme emotions, whether happy or sad, excited or depressed, are much more likely to be noticed than the state of balance and equilibrium. The interesting experience of emotional balance is that it does not demand much of our attention and it does not attract the attention of others.

In Chapter 9 I described how some behaviors come about in order to keep one's attention turned on. Movement can be used to keep our attention awake and to keep us focused. Some people talk as a way of keeping their attention button in the "on" position. I suggest that emotions, and the subsequent behavior caused by emotions, can also serve to keep attention in the alert and "on" position. A temper tantrum in a small child, frantic energy in a school-aged child, or a fit of anger in an adult might all be mechanisms used to keep faltering attention and energy turned up to a higher level. One student told me the reason he was always interrupting in class and talking with his friends was because he felt like he would fall asleep otherwise. For him, he needed to turn off his inhibition button in order to stay engaged. If he inhibited his behaviors, his attention would simply shut down, so he by-passed his inhibition switch in order to stay charged up, active, and engaged, even if it meant that he interrupted inappropriately. A parent said that she would get angry as a way of charging up her attention and energy. The problem with this scenario was that although her anger would charge her up and get her going, everyone around her was suffering. It looked like this adult could take a lot of initiative and accomplish a great deal, but the effect this method had on those around her was more negative than positive. She thought she was controlling her emotions and behaviors just fine, but the people around her became casualties.

It is clear that the executive functions are intertwined, and making a distinct separation between the different functions is not really possible. But it is just because they are so interwoven, and because the ingredients might be applied to aid the strengthening of each function, that we can use the ingredients list again to help make this executive function more understandable.

Control of one's behavior and control of one's emotions can only arise out of a very personal, inner place. In nearly every chapter so far I have mentioned that you cannot change a person purely from the outside. Education of any kind needs to arise from inside the individual, through personal volition, coming from personal initiative, based on personal control. You cannot control another person's behavior, and you cannot control another person's emotions. They might have a specific reaction or response to your behavior or emotions, but you are not able to control them.

Applying some of the ingredients to control of behavior and control of emotion

Relationship

No matter how close your relationship is with another person, you cannot take over this executive control for that person. The nature of the relationship between the student and another person might actually be the cause of an emotional imbalance. If the nature of the relationship is one of trust and empathy, then the emotional and behavioral response is likely to be balanced and calm. If there is stress or distrust between the two people, then the response is likely to be one of anxiety and irritation, or even fear. Fixing the relationship will have a direct effect on the behavior and emotions of the student and it is much more likely to have a positive effect.

Strengths and weaknesses

The ability to control emotions and behaviors is naturally easier if it is in an area of strength. If the student feels confident about a situation, control of emotion and behavior in relation to that situation is fairly easy to achieve. If the situation is one that the student does not feel confident about, then it is likely to elicit fear, anxiety, and possibly an outburst of negative behavior. So it is easier for the good math student to have a steady, emotional response to making a mistake on a math test. If that same student is dyslexic, and makes a language-based mistake so that her language teacher criticizes her weaknesses, she is very likely to have a strong emotional reaction to being treated so poorly by her language teacher. She will not be able simply to ignore the criticism, and will most likely be disproportionately upset by the criticism. In this moment, the negative reaction to the criticism will outweigh the support offered by the kind words from a friend.

Self-advocacy to self-responsibility

It is hard for students to advocate for their needs if their emotions are out of control. Emotional imbalance makes it hard to assess one's immediate needs, and outside interventions are sometimes needed to calm a situation down enough for the student to recognize what their needs actually are. Since controlling one's behavior is needed before, during, and after events, how was the individual engaged with thinking about the behavior, feeling about the behavior, and what was the actual action? What are the conscious and unconscious behaviors? Emotions are often what lie between the thought and the will, so emotions and behavior are intertwined and cannot be controlled as independent experiences.

Preview and review

Review or reflection on behavior and emotion is one of the most powerful tools available for setting up a new decision leading to changes in behavior. The more mature the student, the better he or she is able to think about emotions and behavior reflectively. Reflection can often calm the situation down enough for preview to take place, and for the student to decide what to do next. Since reflection needs a calm environment, those around the student have to calmly withdraw sufficiently to allow the student to decide what to do next. This is especially true for older students who are mature enough to make personal decisions and choices. Younger children still need to be guided through the review and preview process in order to bring calm to emotions and behavior, but it is still possible to speak quietly with them and talk about options.

Motivation and incentive

In relation to control of emotions and behavior it is important to remember about motivation and incentive. Motivation arises from within the student, and will play into behavior and emotion easily. It is advisable to avoid using threats of punishments or promises of rewards as a means of controlling emotions and behavior.

Rather than attempting to control a student from the outside, here are some ideals for guiding the student to learn how to control his or her own emotions and behavior:

- Self-expression: help the student find ways to express his or her feelings in proportion to the events that caused them.

- Self-control: students should be helped to manage emotions in relation to over- or under-reactions to events and to people around them. This is where it is excellent if the teacher and parent can model how to respond, rather than react.

- Self-knowledge: the student can be guided to develop an understanding of the impact he or she has on others. Help the student develop an understanding of how others feel that is similar to how they want to be understood.

Review

Instead of trying to control a student's behavior and emotion from the outside, lead him or her to the capacity for self-directed control through teaching self-expression, self-control, and self-knowledge.

Chapter 16

Goals

Preview

- All executive activity requires goal setting. At times it is inherent or implicit in the activity, at other times it needs to be very explicit.

- Goals can be short-term, intermediate, and/or long-term. There can also be immediate and general goals. When something needs to happen, but it isn't going to get done by itself, it helps to set a goal. Goals help modify behavior in order to achieve the desired result.

Goals come in all sizes and are set for all sorts of reasons. When we refer to setting goals in relation to executive function, it can mean something as small as deciding to wash the dishes, or as big as beginning a four-year college degree. As with all the other executive functions, setting goals is a very personal matter, arising from within the individual as another form of expressing personal volition; or goals can be more public and related to the group we are with. But all executive activity requires some goal setting. Whether they are inherent or implicit in the activity, or explicit and clearly stated, goals are a natural function of our executive functions.

Setting goals can start with simply stating the obvious. You have math homework to do, and you decide to get started, set a timer for 15 minutes, and see how far you are at the end of that time period. Your goals in this case are to get your homework finished and to use a specific period of time to work. Both goals are easily set and easily met.

A slightly more complex set of goals is needed if you have to complete a long-term project. First, you need an overview of the whole project, and then you can see what the parts of the project might contain (whole to parts). Through this preview of the work to come, you are able to identify what is needed as an approach or a system of working. At this point, you start setting goals for the various portions of the project. The first portion will have a time-frame, and a goal for the work to be completed within that time. Then there might be sub-goals within that one larger goal, such as the goal of getting to the library for some research by the end of the first week. The sections of the project will all contain these mini-goals, which in the end will all add up to the main and overarching goal of completing the long-term project on time. Just starting out and telling yourself that you will be ready on time is too big a goal for most people to successfully meet, and it is too vague. Executive functions are supported and trained through the many details that make up something as simple as a goal for the work that is to be accomplished in the first week of a project.

When we review previous experiences, weigh them against the current situation, and make a new decision based on what we have learned, we are engaging not just in decision-making, we are setting goals. Since goals are the achievement we direct our energy toward, making a decision and setting a goal can at times appear very similar. The process to arrive at the decision is even similar to the process for setting goals.

Ideally, having a goal can guide us toward a chosen result, give us parameters to work within, and give structure to our activity. Goals can also become rigid and unyielding. If we set a goal and cannot be free of that goal even when it is no longer relevant, then we become trapped. In this case it is important to set very small goals, in order to avoid getting fixed or stuck in the idea of having to meet that very targeted goal. One area of activity where I see this happening frequently is when students play computer games. Their goal is to win one game, beat their opponent, achieve a certain score, or even just play for a few minutes. Once the game begins, it is very difficult to remember the original goal, and even harder to stop just because someone tells them to.

Setting goals

Short-term goals can be set and accomplished in a short period of time. There can be many short-term goals as component parts of one larger goal, as in the example of the long-term project. The short-term goal can also stand on its own, such as the goal of making the bed, or putting the books on the bookshelf so they can be found when they are needed.

Intermediate goals can be set and accomplished in the near future, in a month, or a week. They can also form a part of a longer-term goal, or stand alone as a single goal. Intermediate goals might be set as a goal to work out in the gym five days out of seven, or to finish your homework every evening before using the computer for fun, or to get your schoolbag packed before going to bed each night for a month. Intermediate goals are often stretched over more than a day, and might require an action to be repeated. An intermediate goal might also be simply to get a certain grade in a class at school. That particular type of intermediate goal will be composed of many smaller, short-term goals in order to be successful.

Long-term goals are set for a longer process, to be met over time—such as goals for a school year, goals for future education, and goals for personal growth and development.

After the goal is identified, try to set some time limits for reaching that goal. Long-term goals will likely include sub-lists of intermediate and short-term goals in order to be successful. Long-term goals need to be realistic, and they often need the input of other people in order to succeed. But we all need long-term goals and we also need to review them occasionally to determine if we are still moving in the right direction.

When following the steps below, be sure to include only what is personally needed to reach the goal. (Although it does happen, it is more difficult when the individual has to depend on someone else in order to meet the responsibilities in relation to the goal.) Remember to incorporate what is known about the student's learning strengths and natural abilities.

1. Identify the goal, and state if it is a short-term, intermediate, or a long-term goal.

2. Identify the steps needed and set the steps out in a logical manner.

- What naturally comes first, middle, or last?

- Arrange complimentary activities.

3. Turn steps into lists, checklists, rules.

- What do I need as tools or supplies?

- What do I need in terms of time?

- What do I need in terms of ideas?

- What steps do I need to follow to reach the goal?

- Do I need help from anyone else?

4. What can prevent you from setting and reaching your goal?

- procrastination

- lack of conviction that the goal needs to be met

- lack of commitment to succeed

- disinterest—leading to lack of commitment

- rebellion—arising when a goal is imposed from the outside

- fear and/or anxiety

- skill deficit

- lack of necessary support.

Taking note of all the details and all the steps involved in setting goals can be very enlightening and very helpful. Over time, the student might not need to put quite so many goals down on paper and track them in this manner, but if goals are tracked explicitly in this way at least initially, then the student has the opportunity to learn how goal setting works for him or her, and in what ways it might be improved over time.

Review

Using executive functions is synonymous with setting and meeting goals. Whether they are inherent or implicit in the activity, or explicit and clearly stated, goals are a natural function of our executive functions. We use executive function in every step of the goal-setting and the goal-meeting process. Setting and meeting goals, then, is a wonderful practice ground for strengthening executive function.

PART III
Practice and Application

At this point in the process of learning how to take personal control of executive functions, it is possible to consolidate what has been learned, and to integrate the new insights into everyday experiences. The student has come to a more defined understanding their personal executive functions, and has become more skilled at identifying the best way to be master of their learning process. The knowledge and understanding about executive functions meets practical applications based on insight and understanding. In the Introduction, the concept of "cohesion" was introduced, and through applying the ingredients to the executive functions, the "cohesion" triad of comprehensibility, meaningfulness, and manageability finally becomes complete. The students become more able to effectively use their executive functions because they experience the integration, or the union, of their thinking, feeling, and actions.

CHAPTER 17

The Executive Function Map

Once the student has learned about each of the executive functions, and has learned to draw from the ingredients to develop strategies and understanding, then he or she can draw out a personal "executive function map." This map has "strengths," "weaknesses," "goals," and "strategies" for each executive function. The map can be drawn initially, and then redrawn a few months later. Maps drawn at intervals to allow for change can serve as pathways or guides for growth and development of learned skills, strategies, and plans for personal executive function.

My executive function map

Attention	Memory	Organization: space	Planning: time
• Strengths • Weaknesses • Goals • Strategies	• Strengths • Weaknesses • Goals • Strategies	• Strengths • Weaknesses • Goals • Strategies	• Strengths • Weaknesses • Goals • Strategies
Initiative and inhibition	Flexibility and/ or shift	Control of behavior and emotion	Goals
• Strengths • Weaknesses • Goals • Strategies	• Strengths • Weaknesses • Goals • Strategies	• Strengths • Weaknesses • Goals • Strategies	• Strengths • Weaknesses • Goals • Strategies

The following examples are gathered from students aged 12–22. These students came from a variety of backgrounds and schools, and participated in workshops, tutoring sessions, or school programs on the theme of "Organization and Study Skills—Executive Function."

Attention

- **Strengths:**
    - When I am paying attention, I can do so for a long period of time.
    - I pay attention easily when I am listening.
    - I pay attention better when it is visual attention.
    - I pay attention well when I am interested.
- **Weaknesses:**
    - It is hard for me to begin paying attention.
    - Colors distract me.
    - I can't read when there is sound near me, I get distracted by noise.
    - I can only read when I listen to music at the same time.
    - I can't pay attention when I am not interested.
    - I can't sit for long and still pay attention.
- **Goals:**
    - Be able to focus better and more easily.
    - Listen to a lecture without tuning out.
    - Be able to read and focus, no matter what situation I am in.
    - Listen in class even if my friends are there.
- **Strategies:**
    - Try to tune out everything else I hear besides what I am supposed to be listening to, and focus better.

- ⊚ Always have a quiet room to work in.

- ⊚ Always have music to listen to while I am working.

- ⊚ Sit up front where I can't see my friends.

- ⊚ Take notes to keep me focused.

- ⊚ Fiddle with something so I can keep myself from being jumpy.

Memory

- **Strengths:**
  - ⊚ Active working memory.
  - ⊚ Long-term memory.
  - ⊚ I have a photographic memory.
  - ⊚ I remember stuff that is interesting to me.
  - ⊚ I remember what I see.

- **Weaknesses:**
  - ⊚ I can only remember when I think the end is near.
  - ⊚ I forget what people say really fast.
  - ⊚ I remember everything, even things I don't need to remember.

- **Goals:**
  - ⊚ To figure out the important stuff to remember.
  - ⊚ To study enough to remember facts.

- **Strategies:**
  - ⊚ Review and preview.
  - ⊚ Repetition.
  - ⊚ Study with my friends.
  - ⊚ Flashcards work for me.
  - ⊚ Write more stuff down.

Organization: space

- **Strengths:**
  - I always know where my stuff is.
  - I am really organized.
  - I keep my papers organized, even if my room is a mess.
- **Weaknesses:**
  - I forget where I put things.
  - I don't have a good system for organization.
  - I am so over-organized my friends tease me about being compulsive.
- **Goals:**
  - Create a good filing system that works for me.
  - Put my school things in the same place every day.
  - Use my visual learning strength to color-code my files.
- **Strategies:**
  - Sometimes I purge everything and start over with less to organize.
  - Organize my school stuff so I don't keep losing my homework.

Planning: time

- **Strengths:**
  - I am really good at long-term projects.
  - I am better with short-term assignments.
  - I like being on time for everything and am usually finished early.

- **Weaknesses:**
  - I am really bad at meeting future deadlines.
  - I am always late for everything.
  - I procrastinate a lot.
  - I always think I have more time than I really have.
  - I don't like using a timer or clock.
- **Goals:**
  - Work on setting some strategies so I can stop being late to everything.
  - Have a visible calendar of my plan so I can see it easily when I need it.
- **Strategies:**
  - Set a calendar as a time-line for my work.
  - Write down my plans for a long-term project.
  - Have my mom help me because she is really good at planning.
  - Use a timer whenever I can.

Inhibition and initiative

- **Strengths:**
  - I can get started easily on something if I am motivated.
  - I can start anything I am interested in doing.
  - I can stop myself when I understand the reason.
- **Weaknesses:**
  - I can barely get myself going.
  - I hate doing things just because I am told to do it.
  - If I really want to do something then no one can make me stop.

- **Goals:**
  - ⊚ To do something even if I don't really want to.
  - ⊚ To find my motivation for what I am supposed to do, so it is easier to do.
- **Strategies:**
  - ⊚ Think things through so it is easier to know why I am doing it.
  - ⊚ Get help to get started so I don't get too stuck.
  - ⊚ Remind myself why I need to stop myself from reacting.

Flexibility and/or shift

- **Strengths:**
  - ⊚ I can easily shift from one activity to another.
  - ⊚ I can think about a lot of things at the same time.
  - ⊚ I am pretty flexible.
  - ⊚ I don't mind having more than one thing going at a time.
- **Weaknesses:**
  - ⊚ I am too flexible, so I don't know when to set a limit.
  - ⊚ I really don't want to shift from one thing to another— once I get started I want to stay with it until it is done.
  - ⊚ I can change what I am thinking, but not what I am doing.
  - ⊚ I am opinionated and think everyone should be like me.
- **Goals:**
  - ⊚ To be able to make changes when I need to.
  - ⊚ Not to feel so stuck in one thing.
  - ⊚ Not to be quite so flexible.
  - ⊚ Keep an open mind.

- **Strategies:**
  - Remind myself why I need to be flexible—it might be that my friends need me to be flexible.
  - Talk myself through the change so it comes easier to me.
  - Prioritize what I need to do.

Control of behavior and emotion

- **Strengths:**
  - I am very composed.
  - My behavior is pretty calm and predictable.
  - People around me say I am predictable.
  - I can handle it pretty well when things don't go my way.
  - I have my feelings pretty well under control.

- **Weaknesses:**
  - Sometimes, without meaning to, I can be pretty rude and mean.
  - I never know what emotion I am feeling.
  - I am very sensitive.
  - I cause a lot of drama around me.
  - I have my feelings too well under control.
  - When things don't happen the way I want, it really upsets me.

- **Goals:**
  - To be nicer to people.
  - Be calmer, more reliable.
  - Not to be so impulsive.
  - Not to let things get me so upset.

- **Strategies:**
  - To think about what I am going to say before I say it.
  - Remind myself before an event about how I want to deal with it.
  - Give myself some more time between a situation and my reaction.
  - Tell people I need time to process, so I don't feel like I have to come up with a quick reaction to something.

Goals

- **Strengths:**
  - I am good at setting short-term goals.
  - I feel like I can plan for long-term goals pretty well.
  - I love having goals because it keeps me focused.
- **Weaknesses:**
  - I have trouble with long-term goals.
  - My short-term goals are so short-term that I have moved on before I get them done.
  - I am more of an "ignore my goals" person.
- **Goals:**
  - To set a good goal, and then meet it.
  - To learn how to set, and plan for, a long-term goal.
  - To take my goals more seriously.
- **Strategies:**
  - Write my goals down so I can't pretend I didn't set them.
  - Tell someone about my goals so they can help me remember how to meet them.
  - Only set little, realistic goals until I learn how to do it better.

Writing an executive function map gives students an opportunity to gain an overview of how they are doing. Students need to be reminded that it is important to change only one thing at a time. Once the individual executive function map is completed, the student can take a step back to see what is working well for him or her and what is still in need of some attention. It is often less overwhelming when they can see what is needed in a wider context. The executive function map actually provides the student with a streamlined summary that is manageable.

Golden rules

At the end of a workshop, series of tutoring sessions, or school-based course, I provide the students with a list of "golden rules" for executive function. The list I use often looks something like this:

Golden rules

- Always work from your strengths.
- Only change one thing at a time.
- Use attention decisions and keep them short enough to stay fresh.
- If attention "fades," turn it back on through movement or a shift in attention.
- Choose a way to support your memory (notes, cards, etc.).
- Organize only the most important things first—don't overwhelm yourself with organizational demands.
- Plan your time using your personal learning style.
- Use preview and review as much as possible.

Guiding principles

- You learn who you are—you cannot easily learn someone else's way.

- Learning has to be understandable, meaningful, and manageable.

- Learning is based on a balance between learning through thinking or cognition, feeling or emotion, and action.

- You are your own best teacher.

Executive function overview

I often provide students with an overview after a series of tutoring sessions ended. This adapted compilation of letters, charts, and plans demonstrates how students work with highly individualized approaches, and how through this model each student is allowed to "learn who they are."

Letter to Brian (18-year-old)

This is a letter to Brian at the conclusion of ten sessions together.

Our weeks of tutoring have come to an end. Although we began by speaking about primarily academic issues, we ended with a more global and inclusive conversation about your learning styles and your approaches to life in general.

The overall goal of the tutoring sessions was to come to insights about your executive functions. The executive functions we targeted were: attention, memory, control of behavior, control of emotions, flexibility, planning (time), organization (space), self-monitoring, and goals. We spoke about each of these, emphasizing attention above all, since that is an area you are consciously working on. For each area, we discussed the elements that make it one of our executive functions, and how you personally experience each of these areas. At about the halfway point, you wrote a kind of "Executive Function Map" that included what you believe to be your strengths, weaknesses, strategies, and goals in each area.

In the early meetings, we spoke about motivation, and you shared that you are motivated by respect. I saw you put this in to practice in several ways. You always related to me respectfully, you spoke about others respectfully, and, most importantly, you appeared to respect yourself. In one of the last sessions we spoke again about motivation, recognizing that you have a great deal of motivation, but you may not always have the tools or skills necessary to implement a given task. That is where our discussion about strategies became very important. What strategy could you use for the situation at hand? We did conclude, though, that you are motivated in two ways: you are *motivated to do*, or to act, and you are *motivated by* events, ideas, etc.

When we worked on memory, you shared that it is hard for you to prioritize. This led to a discussion about how your priorities need to be justified and have a good reason for being chosen for placement in a high priority position. This eventually led to a critical insight, namely that you are the one who needs to set the priority, you are no longer needing or wanting others to tell you how to set your priorities. You are now ready to take responsibility for essential decision-making of this nature.

Attention was a main theme throughout, and we considered several strategies and options for focusing your attention. The attention goal on your EF map started out as: "To be able to rapidly switch my attention to whatever I want." By the end, the goal was expanded to include: "To pace myself in my work, to control when I do things—timing and pace."

In answer to the question, "What do you want to continue to work on or to improve?" you answered:

1. The ability to motivate myself to start any task (like homework) any time.

2. The ability to finish what I start.

3. The ability to choose how I prioritize things.

4. To be able to concentrate on one task for as long as I need to.

5. The motivation to do things I have to do that I don't like, such as review or study.

Then you added that you want to "wake up every morning and enjoy what I do."

You will always be able to recognize your areas of strength, because from your strengths you will derive a sense of purpose, resilience, connectedness, and sense of accomplishment. You have many different areas of strength to draw on when you are confronted by challenges, so keep reminding yourself of your strengths and your strategies. Your best life decisions will be made when you remember your affinities or passions while you are deciding how to implement your strengths.

I hope you find the source within yourself to guide your decisions, organize your priorities, and set your goals for this next phase of your life.

Letter to Ellen (17-year-old)

Ellen worked daily over a concentrated two-week period of time, primarily to improve executive function in her academic setting.

Today we completed our sessions together, and you accomplished a great deal. Our conversations started with an overview of how you see yourself as a learner, and what you experience as your strengths and challenges.

From the first day, you were able to describe what you were feeling and thinking very clearly. You began the week with some good descriptions of who you are as a learner. We talked about how you can try really hard in math and science, but your grades don't reflect how hard you try in these classes. In the education classes, you describe the opposite—that you work hard and have the grades to show for it. You are very interested in the education classes, and that makes it possible for you to maintain your attention and focus. In other classes, as soon as it is not interesting, or you lose the thread of thought, you "zone out" and lose concentration. This theme was one we came back to throughout the week. How can you maintain your focus and concentration even in situations that are not interesting or are challenging academically? You decided to begin by using your learning strengths, such as your strong ability in social interactions and conversations, and your visual learning strength, which can be applied to taking colorful, interesting notes.

A theme running through the whole week was movement! You respond well to movement, it keeps you focused and keeps your brain awake. Whenever you find yourself becoming unfocused, you can take a break and move—and your brain will switch back on.

We spoke about your memory next, and it was initially a mystery why you can remember certain classes perfectly, but can't remember what else happened even a day or two ago. As your learning strengths are both visual and kinesthetic, you can use motor memory and mental visualization as a strategy to help you secure events in your active working memory long enough to move them to your long-term memory.

Your organization skills are applied primarily in the classes that interest you. For those classes your binder is organized and neat, and the information in it is retrievable. This can serve as an example of how other school binders can be organized. At the beginning of the school year, get all your supplies together and choose the supplies that are the most practical. Inner organization and outer organization are linked, so thinking through how you want to organize will support your actual outer organization.

Planning is related to time management, and although you can schedule your activities and use a planner, you don't always know how much time a specific event or task will actually take. When the original planning doesn't work, you have to use flexibility to choose another plan, which is one strategy to use for adjusting to a newly determined plan. Use preview and review liberally throughout your planning process to clarify what you want to do (plan—preview) and how successfully you are accomplishing your goal (review—adjusting plan). Organize as much as you can the night before, and write down all your to-do lists on the whiteboard.

One great tool for time management is to reflect on your day in reverse. Think back through everything that happened, starting with the most recent event and working back to the beginning of the day. This will strengthen your memory, highlight areas in your planning that were successful, and strengthen your capacity to review and reflect.

Your work as a student will be strengthened by getting a large whiteboard, writing your schedule on it, and using it to organize your study. Plot out the material you are studying in some kind of note-taking style (mind map, bubbles, popcorning ideas, lists, outlines, etc.) Once the information is all on the board, you will be able to step back and get an overview of the material you are studying. The usual study style of working at a desk activates the left brain, or the more linear, analytic part of your brain. Working while standing up and using an overview activates the right, more creative and synthesizing part of your brain.

You are beginning to form personal goals, and your academic goals are forming around them. Your goal of studying to become a teacher is an excellent personal goal, and organizing your academic goals to be able to meet the personal goals is perfect. Organizing your schoolwork, using your classroom and personal study time more efficiently, and planning your senior year carefully will all lead you toward your goal of academic success so you can move into the profession of your choosing.

At the conclusion of our sessions, you created a list of action items that will help you work stronger, not harder:

- Use the strength of your personal relationships to maintain interest in your work and to help you focus.

- Put up a large whiteboard, and take notes with colored pens and drawings. Use this for developing an overview when you study.

- Strengthen your focus and concentration—practice the paper clip concentration exercise for 30 seconds at a time. As soon as you can concentrate on absolutely nothing but the paper clip for 30 seconds, increase it to 60 seconds.

- Review your day in reverse to strengthen both memory and organization skills.

- Work from an overview whenever possible.

- Write your schedule down, even to the point of writing down your rhythm of study and taking a break.

- Use the night to prepare for the following day.

- Use preview and review when you plan, when you study, and when you organize.

- Talk things over with family and friends when you are making decisions.

- When working on your own sounds daunting, use your social skills and collaborate with friends to get started on projects.

I am confident in your ability to strengthen your strategies and approaches for organizing your personal and academic life. I wish you the best in all you do.

Letter to Margaret (16-year-old)

This is the letter written for Margaret at the end of ten sessions.

When you first came to tutoring, I asked you what you wanted to achieve through tutoring. You said you wanted to be able to focus better, and you expressed some concern about your grades and your ability to apply yourself to your studies. Over our sessions together we identified your learning styles, learned about your learning strengths and weaknesses, discussed strategies, and implemented new approaches to your studies.

Your learning styles are enhanced by using visuals such as pictures and color. You can draw little depictions of the content and use highlighters to color notes and important texts. You are very connected to movement and writing, which might be why you would prefer to write by hand over using the computer. Using computer programs for graphics and mind-mapping may work well for you because they are based on color, movement, and form.

You are also very musical, and found that if you needed to learn something by memory, making a little song or melody helped you remember. Auditory learning that is language-based is OK for you, but not your first choice, so learning that is primarily auditory language is not optimal for you.

We discovered that several approaches help your memory. We talked about using mnemonics, charts, and the "flipchart" we made together by taping index cards into a manila folder. These approaches seem to work for you because they blend your learning strengths by using visual aids, color, and form.

Organizing your thoughts in relation to a paper, report, or simply to study the content needed some work on overview organization. We strategized about how you can identify main points, main thoughts, and connecting links. We talked about outlines and overviews, and how both help get the main ideas of the material clarified. Knowing how important it is to have an overview of the material, we talked about the strategy of preview and review. To preview the material prepares you for what you will learn, so that when you actually settle in to learn it, it is already familiar. Review uses reflection and reconstruction, to "remember" the material, or put the pieces back together again.

When we started the sessions on attention and memory we uncovered important information about how you learn. You described how difficult it is for you to focus, to be consistent, to maintain momentum, and to prioritize. You also described how hard you work and how little you have to show for it. You are actually studying too hard for the few results you are getting.

So, after creating a chart of your strengths/focus and weaknesses/distractions, we set up a few specific strategies for you to use.

Work smarter, not harder! Use your strengths! Always start with your strengths!

Set a timer:

- 20 minutes—study (Identify the subject and activity ahead, so you are prepared to begin as soon as the time starts.)

- 10 minutes—distraction (Indulge a distraction—they are often relaxing activities.)

- 20 minutes—study

- 10 minutes—distraction

- Repeat as long as necessary to complete the work.

The way to make this strategy successful is to keep to the set times, and not stretch them. You had some success with improved grades during the time of tutoring, and that has great potential to continue. Let structure be your friend, and allow yourself to both focus and be "distracted." This is like breathing in and breathing out. We need both to stay alive, and you need both to keep your brain activated and focused. Concentrate—relax—concentrate—relax, etc.

You made a series of cards listing things you wanted to work on, and out of the five cards, I gave you only one card to work on. Remember, you can't change many things at once. You will be doing well if you can change even one thing, so create realistic and achievable goals for yourself. You will be so pleased when you reach even one goal, and that will inspire you to take on the next one. Keep your goals written down, and review them often. You are the one who knows your learning needs the best. You can trust your instincts, and you can be honest with yourself, so you can try new ideas until you see if they are good strategies for you. By being honest with yourself, you will gradually build a repertoire of strategies that work successfully and specifically for you. That is your main goal. This kind of self-advocacy will lead you to self-responsibility, and there is nothing more thrilling than the feeling of knowing you are guiding your life with wisdom and personal leadership.

I enjoyed all of our sessions, and I wish you success and joy in your learning process in the future.

Letter to Ellisa (14-year-old)

This is the letter to Ellisa who came for tutoring to improve her academic success and strengthen executive function.

You have accomplished an impressive amount of learning and changing in our weeks together. You have organized your space so you can find your books, papers and backpack. You have organized your math so you can look up formulas and important facts as you need them. You have organized your binders for each class and you are able to follow them so you always know what is going on and what your homework is for each day. You have become more aware of your grammar and are able to follow editing comments so your papers are well written.

Also, you are more confident and you smile a lot! When we started, there were many things you said you couldn't do. Now, there are many more things you know you can do. That will make a tremendous difference in your life and your learning path.

You seem to be directing your learning the way you know it will work best for you. That allows you to set up approaches and strategies that will work for you into the future.

You have courageously set and met your goals. That is such an important thing to learn, and you are gaining important experience every time you set a goal.

So, enjoy your successes in learning, and I am very impressed with you and the amount of progress you have made in such a short time.

CHAPTER 18

Specific Approaches

Recommendations for Jim (15-year-old)

This comprehensive chart was written for Jim instead of a narrative letter. We worked collaboratively on the development of all aspects of this chart.

Strategy for all learning

PREVIEW

- What do I need to do today?

- What materials do I need?

- How much time will it take?

- How is my work/content organized?

- What do I need for tomorrow or this week?

REVIEW

- What did I learn?

- How does it connect to what I know?

- How can I remember it so it can help me later?

- What do I need to repeat, rewrite, review?

Setting up a work schedule
MY ATTENTION WANDERS, SO...

1. Work for 10–15 minutes.

2. Take a short "sensory break."

3. Make a *new attention decision.*

- Don't try to go too long in one working session, but make a genuine decision to keep focused for the 10–15 minutes!

- Make sure the breaks include some kind of organized sensory input—for example:

   - Fiddle with a squeeze ball or "fiddleable" item.

   - Move around the desk/room.

   - Drink some water.

   - Talk with an adult to give them an update on your work.

- Keep the sensory break *short* and return to the work in progress.

- Use *flexibility/shift* to go into the break and to make the decision to refocus on the work in hand.

- Self-advocate: I know what I need.

- Self-responsibility: I am responsible to make it happen.

TURN RANDOM THOUGHTS INTO FOCUSED THOUGHTS THROUGH "POPCORNING"

1. Popcorn random thoughts—get them all out there.

2. Focus—prepare to organize these thoughts.

3. Categorize.

4. Identify themes.

5. Get inspired.

6. Identify the big idea.

Do this process in writing, and end with the main theme, big idea, or organized direction.

- Random thoughts are a strength of our creative, *right brain.*

- Linear, organized thoughts are a strength of our organized, *left brain.*

- **We need both.**

Saliency determination

What is important for me to work on and why?

Self-monitoring

How am I really doing? What strategy can get me back in focus if I lose sight of my goals?

Pacing

Am I going too slow? Too fast?

Rhythm and routine

Task	Monday	Tuesday	Wednesday	Thursday	Friday
Morning					
• Homework complete					
• Homework in folders					
• Gym clothes					
School					
• Papers for each class					
• Write in planner for each class					
Home					
• Do homework for each class					
• File *all* papers					
• Prepare backpack for morning					

A brief description of how Jim characterizes his thought process, feelings, and ability to do things

Thinking	Feeling	Will
• Absent-minded professor. • Not thinking about what is in front of me. • Can focus on my own thoughts and not get distracted if it is on my own agenda.	• A train that periodically changes tracks. • Like to be praised. • Can hold a grudge.	• A man who knows that work is necessary, but who would rather be sleeping. • I like to fiddle with papers. • I need to speed up some things and slow down others. • Routine, once established, is difficult for me to change. • Need warnings before activity changes.

Report to the teacher of Cameron (14-year-old)

This report advocates for Cameron to receive some accommodations in his learning environment.

Cameron was referred to me for academic support in math due to ADHD (inattentive type) and weakness in executive function. He also has dyslexia, so processing language presents some challenges to him. Based on our work together, I could recommend the following strategies for Cameron:

- **Time—math:** Although Cameron has average processing speed, he needs extra time to sort out the information that is language-based. For example, when he sees a math problem that is purely numbers, he is able to compute the answer more quickly. If the math problem is inserted into language, he needs more time to understand the written language, create the math problem in numbers, and then solve the problem.

- **Time—language:** Cameron needs a little more time to understand language-based information and differentiate essential from non-essential information. He will be supported by class notes and handouts that are organized with bolded words, bulleted lists that limit the amount of words he has to process, and visual organization that supports meaning in more than a narrative format.

- **Visual and conceptual information:** Switching between the visual and conceptual takes him a bit more time. In tutoring, we practiced computing some of the math problem mentally, and then wrote down only the more complex parts of the math problem. This also helped increase his working speed.

- **Dyslexia and auditory processing:** Because Cameron has dyslexia, he needs more time to process language effectively. He also has some auditory processing challenges, so I recommend that his overall language load be a bit lightened. Try to show him, rather than explain to him, how to approach a problem.

- **Multisensory instruction:** Cameron benefits from instruction that is delivered in more than one way. Verbal instructions that are also written down will be more effective for him, for example. Any time he can engage in learning through multisensory means will support his learning capacity.

- **Study style:** I encourage Cameron to study using more than one style. He can read the material, write down notes, write things up on a whiteboard, talk about the material, move while studying, etc. Maintaining variety in his study styles will help him use his strengths, keep his attention engaged, and prevent him from getting lulled into one way of working.

These suggestions will help with his overall learning style and directly support further development of his executive functions.

Frank (17-year-old)

This is a synopsis of the initial phase of our work together. Frank continues to work on these areas and created specific academic goals from this overview.

Main questions

- What are you looking for?
- What are your learning needs?
- What is your experience of your own learning?

Issues

- Slow processing speed, especially when processing the meaning of written words or when doing mental math.
- Looking for strategies to get around "inane tasks."
- Why and how to approach an issue.

Remember: **Start from your strengths!**

Wants to learn

- Memorization strategies.
- Strategies to be more efficient.
- Better computation/calculation strategies.

Strengths

- Real word problems in math that have meaning and are relevant to real life problems.
- Strong in math, but he has to see it—mental math is not his strength. He has his own way of solving a multiplication/math problem—he breaks it down to tens/hundreds, etc., and calculates from there.

- History—gets the whole picture, can compare/contrast and imagine. Not so good with dates.

- Things need to be relevant—he does his best work when he knows *why* he is doing something.

Challenges

- Teachers matter a great deal—they can't be boring, monotone, or unreasonable.

- He likes teachers to be interesting, open to questions, able to discuss the issues.

Self-advocacy

Frank needs to discover enough about his own learning style to self-advocate for his needs, and to deal with a less-than-perfect situation that might require him to adjust.

Overview of executive function

1. Self-knowledge—a deductive learner, works from an overview first; analysis rather than synthesis as the starting point of strength.

2. Think ahead—have a list ready of what tools will be needed for a test, assignment, etc. Write it down so you can "see" what you have to prepare.

3. Overview your textbooks so you can see what kind of approach is being taken and then decide what you need to fill in the blanks.

4. Identify your own review and preview needs and supplement when the teacher or text doesn't supply enough for you. Review and preview are building blocks for the overview—and the overview is a place of strength for you.

Goals

Your long-term goals are well articulated. We talked about your short-term goals needing more specific parameters and connecting links between short- and long-term goals. We worked on what is needed to turn a short-term goal into a long-term goal.

Memory tips

- Strategies for linking short-term and long-term memory:
  - lists
  - notes, tables, graphs
  - highlight and chunk information
  - visualization
  - verbal recordings
  - repetition, repetition, repetition, repetition, repetition, repetition, repetition…
  - self-talk when needed.
- Biggest challenges and obstacles this last year:
  - social
  - distractions (mainly social)
  - reactions to teachers
  - lazy—are you really lazy or does something else stop you from getting to the work? If it is social, you can't change other people—you can only change yourself. How might that be done?
- Self-knowledge is a private matter, so this is something only you can do for yourself. You can know that:
  - You only have control over your own experience, no matter how others behave.
  - Others, especially teachers, won't have the same vested interest in your success.

⊛ You would do well with a list of triggers to watch out for.

Anna (15-year-old)

This chart for Anna was given to her in the form of small cards that she could use one at a time to remind herself of her goals, decisions, and successes.

Initiative	Flexibility	Attention
• Decide what needs to be done and get started without having to be asked or reminded.	• Adapt to various situations by shifting focus and pace as the situation unfolds.	• Focus long and accurately enough to learn important information. • Block distractions. • Prioritize information.
Organization	**Planning**	**Working memory**
• Manage space and things. • Organize your binder, your books, your daily schedule, and your working space at school and at home.	• Plan your time—so you can start your projects at the right time and finish on time. • A good plan will make it possible to live by the saying, "timing is everything!"	• Retain information long enough to store it in your long-term memory. Working memory is pervasive—and all learning is based on it. • A good example: Remember what your assignments are and when they are due!!
Self-awareness	**Managing emotions**	**Five points of the Star of Success**
• Sufficient "self-knowledge." • See yourself as others see you. • Know how to act in order to avoid unintended consequences.	• Express your feelings in proportion to the event that elicited them. • Notice when you are in or out of sync with those around you. • Respond to life, rather than react to life.	1. Excellent binder organization—established and maintained! 2. All late assignments turned in for credit. 3. All new assignments turned in on time. 4. Increased confidence in self as a learner. 5. Increased ability to plan. Can better foresee expectations and consequences. CONGRATULATIONS!

Practical strategies for implementing improvement in executive function

The following is a synopsis of a conversation with a college-aged student. This demonstrates how chosen principles from the work with executive function can be implemented in a practical situation:

English

You missed two classes by choice and one class due to the weather. At first you said you missed the two classes because you are lazy, but I don't think that is the real reason. Remember our conversation about the difference between your personal motivation and laziness? What does motivate you to do well in this class? You described the teaching in English class as focused on the book discussion, and the regular writing assignments. Rather than be uninspired by this teacher, take personal control of your learning environment. Remember, the motivation and inspiration to do well lies within yourself, and within your control.

Decisions:

- Speak directly with the teacher, asking for an overview of the goals and intentions of the course to ensure that you are not missing anything vital.

- Write your own responses to the readings in advance, changing them before you hand them in as needed. This will be an excellent exercise in preview/review.

- Provide your own interest and initiative rather than wait for the teacher to inspire you and guide your actions in relation to class work.

Math

Despite knowing the concepts well, and completing the take-home test accurately, the grade was still 68 percent. We went over the math test and identified a few things the teacher marked you down for, and they were most often process errors or writing errors, not overall concept and understanding errors. You made some decisions about how to improve this.

Decisions:

- Talk directly with the teacher and ask why each one was marked down, so avoidable mistakes don't have to be made.

- Establish with your teacher that you will get extra time for math tests, so you can have time to go over a test and catch as many details as possible.

Business Class I

You are keeping up with the reading and taking good notes in class. The teacher hasn't given a time-line for the four exams that make up the grade for this course. In order to prepare for that exam, you might write up your notes in color on a large piece of paper. This will reinforce the learning through writing it again, and it will establish "memory hooks" by using colors, organization of the notes, and rewriting them.

Decisions:

- Rewrite, reorganize your class notes as a way of studying them.

- Create memory hooks in as many ways as possible.

Business Class II

The teacher liked your idea for your "elevator pitch." You will still work on a class idea while working on the business plan for the new idea. This is more work than expected, but it is also interesting and fun.

Decisions:

- This is an assignment where you can use your strength of working well with others.

- Keep a written record of how your ideas evolve, so you can give an accounting of why you made each decision along the way.

CHAPTER 19
Conclusion
Golden Rules

At the end of many sessions or workshops, I ask the students to identify their "take-away" from the work we did. What did they find either meaningful or interesting? What did they learn that made learning more comprehensible? What did they learn that would make their life more manageable?

The answers from the students are remarkably clear and direct, and the answers can also be somewhat unexpected, and even surprising. During this reflection time, we work together to gather the most salient points that we covered, and identify a way to put the new learning into practice. Now that the student has an overview of the issues, and a deeper understanding of the ideas, it is a good time to identify their personal, individualized strategies.

The sum of everything that was covered in all our meetings is simply too much to process and remember at once. In order to focus attention on the most important details, or the most memorable new ideas, the student might make a little "cheat sheet" of reminders, small enough to remember, and written down so it can be posted in a visible place. In the beginning of our sessions, we have conversations about attention at the hand of those two important questions: "What do you pay attention to?" and, "What attracts your attention?" These two questions lead the student to most of the insights that follow, since so many of their experiences are, in essence, an expression of how they use attention. Understanding how to use these insights and apply them in daily life will eventually lead to the important changes in how they use their attention.

The one area that is not previously addressed in this book is the use of technology. The current debate related to what is good technology or bad technology, what is enough or what is too much, is not what this book is about. There is excellent research available about the use of technology and its effects on children. There is also growing interest in the effects of video games and general technology use specifically on attention span, learning difficulties, and emotional stress. As much as possible, I encourage parents and students to understand their own use of technology in relation to making it a learning support rather than a hindrance.

The following are samples of these strategies and reminders for the student.

Always work from your strengths

Everyone has strengths. List yours here so you can easily remember what they are, and make it easier to remind yourself what you do well. Beginning by identifying even just one, and you can build on your list of strengths over time. Here are some ideas to get you thinking about your own strengths. You might find you have strengths in each of these areas of *thinking, feeling,* and *action.*

Thinking

- Strong in certain subjects—science, math, language arts, history, foreign language, etc.

- Can understand concepts easily.

- Good at putting thoughts in writing, or good at talking them through.

Feeling

- Can be a good friend.

- Understands nuance or implicit ideas.

- Comfortable with artistic expression.

Action

- Prefer to make a project rather than write a paper.

- Comfortable with learning-by-doing.

- Can take good notes—but might need to draw and doodle during the process.

Only change one thing at a time

Too often I hear parents and teachers list a long series of issues and grievances that add up to the sum of what is "wrong" with the student. Asking a student to change all the things on that long, long list of wrongs is an impossible task. One pedagogical law that I have always adhered to is that you can and should only change one thing at a time.

Identify one thing you want to change, and keep the first thing really small and achievable. Gigantic goals are scary and most people cannot face them. Who makes a long list of New Year's resolutions and actually keeps them all? Most people do not succeed at keeping resolutions, and just making a longer list will not ensure success. Choose something small and give yourself an achievable time-frame to practice the change. As the first change is successfully met, gradually add to your list of changes.

Some ideas of small changes

- Decide to put your backpack in a certain place every day.

- Keep a file in your binder for homework only.

- Prepare your materials for school the night before.

- Use colored pens when taking notes.

- Check online for posted assignments every evening.

- Go to bed 30 minutes earlier on school nights.

- Plan your project out on a calendar and set the schedule to match your learning strengths.

- Practice preview and review every day for a week and see if it helps with focus and orientation.

The list of potential things to change is endless. Just remember: start small and be content with one change at a time.

Use technology as a tool, not a crutch

- Decide if using an electronic calendar is a good idea for you.

- If you do use an electronic calendar, sync it where possible with parents, teachers, or other calendars that are relevant to your work.

- Decide where you will enter assignments and projects and be consistent about it.

- Use the internet as a research tool, in addition to physical copies from libraries, etc. Be able to work with both mediums.

- Use texting and email as an effective tool for communication and being in touch. These can also be great distractions, so once you make your decision how best to use these options, write it down so you can't trick yourself into forgetting what you decided. The better you are able to decide how to work with these electronic choices, the less your teachers and parents will decide for you.

- Write on the computer if it is a more efficient option for you, especially if you are an older student who has already mastered the art of handwriting. If you do choose the computer, make good use of the editing capabilities, but remember the computer can only edit what you write.

Use attention decisions and keep them short enough to keep them fresh

- Remember to use shorter attention decisions.

- Work for a short time, take a break, then start fresh on a new work session.

- Work for ten minutes, take a two-minute break, and repeat as often as needed.

- Change up the time you work and the length of the break. Track what works best for you. No one else will know better than you how to manage your attention decisions.

If attention "fades," turn it back on through movement or a shift in attention

- Movement will always turn your attention back on.

- Sit on a big ball rather than a chair when studying.

- Have tennis balls available to roll under your feet as a way of keeping alert.

- Use "fiddle items" if your hands are free.

- Chew gum while studying.

- Stand up, stretch, run around, jump up and down.

- Occasionally, lie down to read.

- Yoga positions and yoga movements can turn your attention switch back on.

Saliency determination (to determine what is important)

This phrase is easy to remember because it is so unique. After we discussed what this might mean to you, it was time for you to identify what is salient, or important, in a school setting, in relation to friends, in the content of a reading passage, in your own feelings, etc. The options are endless, and you are always in a process of determining what is salient in a given moment. Remember how important and pervasive saliency determination is in everyday life. Make saliency determination a priority for yourself.

Choose a way to support your memory

No two memories work exactly the same, so there are no memory-strengthening strategies that will work exactly the same for everyone. Make your memory strategy decision based on your learning strengths, and try more than one if you are not sure what will work for you.

- Flashcards—use color if that is a help.

- Rewrite your notes—if you want to change up the style, if you initially took handwritten notes, rewrite them on the computer. If you took them on the computer, rewrite the outline as handwritten notes. Otherwise, rewrite them in the format you initially took them in, and improve on the important details or information. The key here is that rewriting notes in any form can strengthen memory and aid recall.

- Use audio support for your learning—read what you need to study into a recorder, and play it back as a memory tool if you are an auditory learner.

- Write what you need to memorize on a big sheet of paper on the wall.

- Use highlighters to keep visual track of what you need to remember.

- Talk out loud to yourself.

- Memorize to rhythm or music.

- Study in more than one setting—the change of setting may provide more "memory hooks."

Organize only the most important things first—don't overwhelm yourself with organizational demands

- Organize one area at a time. What will you choose as a starting point? Your binder? Your papers? Your backpack? Your desk? Your locker at school? Your note-taking style? Your thoughts? It is important that whatever you choose to organize becomes a support to you.

- Plan your time using your personal learning style.

- Your personality is an important ally in deciding how to plan and use your time.

- Decide how you work best. (Hardest job first? Easiest job first? Front to back? Start with an overview and work toward the details? Start with the details and work toward an overview?)

- Get an overview of the time available before you decide how you want to spread the work out. You might like to "front load" the work and get as much as possible done at the beginning. You might prefer to leave it to the end and get it done under pressure when you are close to the deadline.

- Know what the positives and negatives are for your planning choices. If you like to front load, do you have a hard time picking it up again at the end? Have you forgotten what the project was about by that stage? If you like to leave everything to the last minute, will your work suffer? What do you do when you find new information and need a bit of time to research it before adding it—but you have run out of time because you started so close to the due date?

- Once you decide how to plan your time, follow through. At the end of the project, reflect on how your choices worked for you and decide if you want to make that choice again. Planning is one element of executive function, but reflecting and adjusting is also an important element of executive function.

Use preview and review as much as possible

- This is one of the most powerful tools you have available for strengthening executive function.

- Look ahead to the coming day. If you do this at night, you have a better chance of having your materials and assignments prepared and ready to go. You will also have a chance to sleep on your preview, making you much more ready for the coming day. Any time you preview a day, a lesson, a meeting, or a test, you are creating receptivity in your brain. The situation you previewed is then experienced as familiar territory.

- Review can also be used in many ways. Reread the passage, review your notes, think back on what you heard, etc.

- The most powerful review tool is to go over your day backward. Think back on the day, but totally in reverse. You can even rewind it in your mind, like a movie going backwards. This will have a powerful effect on how you can recapture salient experiences, recall important details, and on how you feel integrated in experiences that make up your day. This strengthens executive function on nearly every level. Go over it backwards!

Use as many outer supports as you can

- Stand up to do your work—write on board, write on a paper taped on the wall. One student painted her walls with blackboard paint and was able to keep her work in a master system on the wall, easily visible and easily adapted. It doesn't matter how you do it, just get up and write. You will remember it better, see it better, and it will be easier to recall the information when you need it.

- Keep two tennis balls handy and roll them under your feet to keep your attention focused.

Music and your playlist

Playing music when you study is a personal choice. For some with ADHD, it can serve as an aid to "keep the attention switch turned on." For others, playing music is a huge distraction.

- If music helps you when you study, play music when you study.

- If music distracts you when you study, don't play music when you study.

- If you do play music, choose the kind that helps you most. Do you like music with words or without words? Do you like a strong beat or a gentle rhythm? Do you like it loud or quiet? These are very personal decisions, and your answer might change, depending on what you are studying, where you are, and who you are with.

- As a memory aid, make a playlist of five or six of your favorite songs. Make one for each subject. Whenever you do your math homework, for example, play your math playlist. This way, when you are in a quiet room taking a math test, your playlist will automatically start playing in your head, and you will not only remember the material more easily, you will also feel like your music is "playing" and it will help you stay focused during the test.

Guiding principles

- You learn who you are—you cannot easily learn someone else's way.

- Learning has to be understandable, meaningful, and manageable.

- Learning is based on a balance between learning through thinking (or cognition), feeling (or emotion), and action.

- You are your own best teacher.

All of these "take-away" ideas and suggestions are highly individualized for each student. The reason they have worked in so many situations is because the student went through a process of discovery that resulted in personal insight. The ideas here are not recipes. Each student had the ingredients available and came up with some combination of strategies, ideas, and insights which led that student to be able to formulate his or her "take-away." The student used what was personally true and put that into a workable plan; no one can actually do this for the student. The student had the voice. The student used that voice.

Although each student takes a different path toward the goal, the goal is to:

- Make learning more comprehensible or understandable so the student can work out of the strengths in his or her thinking.

- Make learning more meaningful or relevant, so the student can work out of the strengths in his or her feelings.

- Make learning more manageable or successful, so the student can work out of the strengths in his or her action or will.

Every approach in this book points toward starting from the positive perspective. Rather than assume the student's attention is broken and needs to be fixed, it works so much better to "fix our attention" on the changes the student is capable of, and on the skills the student can already bring to the process. Starting from a point of abundance rather than deficit encourages excitement for the process of growing, developing, and learning—for the teachers and parents, as well as the students. This is how we can achieve the "attention fix."

References

Antonovsky, A. (1987) *Unraveling the Mystery of Health: How People Manage Stress and Stay Well*. San Francisco, CA: Jossey-Bass.

Barkley, R. (2005) *Taking Charge of ADHD: The Complete Authoritative Guide for Parents*. New York: Guilford Publications.

Barkley, R. (2010) *Taking Charge of Adult ADHD*. New York: Guilford Press.

Buonomano, D. (2011) *Brain Bugs: How the Brain's Flaws Shape Our Lives*. New York: W.W. Norton and Co.

Carr, N. (2010) *The Shallows: What the Internet is Doing to our Brains*. New York: W.W. Norton and Co.

Davidson, C.N. (2011) *Now You See It: How the Brain Science of Attention will Transform the Way We Live, Work, and Learn*. New York: Viking–Penguin Group.

Dewey, J. (2005) *Democracy and Education*. (Reprint.) New York: Free Press.

Doidge, N. (2007) *The Brain that Changes Itself: Stories of Personal Triumph from the Frontiers of Brain Science*. New York: Penguin Group.

Eisner, E. (2002) *The Arts and the Creation of Mind*. New Haven, CT: Yale University Press.

Fox, J. (2009) *Your Child's Strengths: A Guide for Parents and Teachers*. New York: Viking.

Lavoie, R. (2007) *The Motivation Breakthrough*. New York: Touchstone/Simon & Schuster.

Levine, M. (2002) *A Mind at a Time*. New York: Simon & Schuster.

Vygotsky, L.S. (2006) *Mind in Society: The Development of Higher Psychological Processes*. A collection of Vygotsky's papers edited by M. Cole, V. John-Steiner, S. Scribner and E. Souberman. Cambridge, MA: Harvard University Press.

Index